Chasing the Story

by David Whisenant

Dedication

I DEDICATE THIS BOOK, AS I HAVE DEDICATED my life, to God. God made it possible for me to have the career that I've had and gave me certain abilities and gifts that were well-suited to the job of a television news reporter. Along with reporting news, I've been able to sit and talk and pray with people who were in the most difficult circumstances they would ever face.

To Jtan, thank you for putting up with so much for so long, for always encouraging me, and for keeping the faith. To Kyle, Anna, Ava, Maisie, and Lucy, thank you for filling in the full picture of a loving and supportive family. Thank you to my mom and daddy, brother Chris, and sister Pam.

Now that the easy part of the dedication is out of the way, I'll get to the difficult part. Thanking God and my family is obvious, but after that my mind runs lap after lap in a literary relay where I can't be sure who to hand the baton off to before we reach the finish line. There are so many hands who have reached out to help me carry the load over the years.

To Karen Wood, Dale Basinger, William Tunstall, Barbara Benton, and many other public school teachers who had to put up with my class clown antics and yet still encouraged me in pursuing my education—thank you. Thank you to my professors at Appalachian State University for opening my mind to new worlds and points of view.

My radio career was filled with people who inspired me. WSTP/WRDX owner Tom Harrell's insistence on excellence even in a small-town radio station largely shaped how I would work as a television reporter. Doug Rice, the well-known voice of NASCAR on the Performance Racing Network, taught me the basics of which buttons to press to have a good show, but also taught me quite a bit about how to be an effective communicator. Kent Bernhardt's flawless delivery on WSTP and the Performance Racing Network was something I always wanted to emulate, and his friendship and encouragement have been a constant in my life for decades.

My television career is filled with dozens of people that I'd like to recognize, but I'm sure I would unintentionally overlook someone, so there's the challenge. Former WBTV anchor and published author Molly Grantham encouraged me to write this book and put me in touch with Betsy Thorpe and Katherine Bartis, who have been indispensable to me in the writing and copyediting that pulls all my thoughts together into the coherent form that you are reading now. Thanks as well to Frazer Dobson and Katie Bogle for help with the proofreading, and Diana Wade for the design of the book and Duncan Blachford for the book's cover design. There have been so many other people at WBTV over the years that have been helpful to me in so many ways—reporters, photographers, anchors, editors, managers, engineers, and more—all contributed to building my career. I can't possibly list them all, but my hope is that I have shown them my appreciation over the years.

Police officers, firefighters, emergency responders, elected officials, public information, and public relations officers are all an important part of my story. I appreciate the patience they showed and the availability they demonstrated to give me an interview or at least answer a few questions as I tried my best to create an accurate news story.

I had the privilege of watching emergency responders in an intimate way as they went about their life-saving tasks. I was often amazed at the efforts they went to in helping those in need, and I always tried to give them due credit when I reported stories in which they played vital roles. We are blessed and fortunate that so many folks accept the calling of public service and stand ready to protect and serve all of us.

I would be remiss if I didn't thank the viewers who ultimately made it possible for me to stay on the air for as long as I did. Thank you for the letters and comments and all the feedback that was sent my way over years. And thank you to all of those people that I approached on city sidewalks and in shopping center parking lots when I had to get that "man on the street" soundbite to include in the story. I did that nearly every day over thirty-two years because I always felt like a story wasn't really complete without the thoughts of the "real people" most directly affected by the subject of the story. Most people were gracious, some ran the other way, and some were downright nasty when I approached them. All played a part in making me the reporter that I became.

Finally, I want to dedicate this book to the late Steve Crump. Crump was my friend and colleague at WBTV and was a nationally recognized journalist and documentary filmmaker. I don't think there's ever been a better storyteller in the Charlotte television market than Steve Crump. He could write a story on a subject that you have no interest in and make you a passionate believer by the time the story was finished. His knowledge of history and human nature gave him the unique ability to understand his subjects at a much deeper level than most journalists. Cancer claimed his life much too early. After his initial diagnosis and his long time off the air, he still called or texted me frequently. Even from his home or hospital bed, he watched the local news and let me know if my story on any particular day was good, or if it was missing something that he thought it needed. I always took his advice. Crump learned that President Reagan's Secret Service name was "Rawhide." Knowing that I admired Reagan, Crump gave me the same nickname. When my phone buzzed and the screen read "Steve Crump," and after I said "Hello," he simply said, "Rawhide . . ." in that deep voice that I so admired. The community he served was a better place because of his work and that's what I strived to create as well. Rawhide will forever be grateful to you, Steve.

Prologue

A firefighter stands by a wrecked car in what is a site often seen by local news reporters.

THEY'RE THOSE THINGS THAT MAKE YOU TAKE your eyes off the road when you're driving. What was that tall column of black smoke that I saw rising in the sky miles and miles away? Why did I see so many police cars all speeding by in the same direction? What happened at the house down the street, and why is it surrounded by yellow tape with words printed in black that say *CRIME SCENE—DO NOT ENTER*? Your local news and your local reporters seek to give you those answers.

It's also the celebration of the local Little League team winning the state championship, the high school student overcoming the odds to win a scholarship, and a person who makes a miraculous recovery from disease or an accident. The new courthouse; Veterans Day and Christmas parades; a ribbon cutting for a pickleball court, interstate highway, or the new factory or mom-and-pop business that will create jobs and offer something new to the community.

Local news is all of this and more, and for thirty-two years, I had a front seat to observe, write about, and present these signature moments. I knew that when I retired, I wanted to write a book to give you a behind-the-scenes look at some significant moments in our community and in my life. I've been blessed over the years to witness so many things, both heartbreaking and celebratory. I want you to see how reporters gather facts and put together the story you watch on your TVs, tablets, laptops, and phones, and I want you to see it from the true boots-on-the-ground perspective.

My day began when the person working at the WBTV News assignment desk would tell me what story or stories I was going to cover on any given day. My assignment for you is to come along with me to the world of local news, as seen through the eyes of someone who grew from a neophyte to a veteran journalist, right in front of a never blinking camera.

1: Erica Parsons I

Erica Parsons

SHE WAS THE LITTLE GIRL THAT FEW people knew, but that everyone would come to know for the way she died at the hands of her caregivers.

On July 30, 2013, a young man named Jamie Parsons, upset with his parents for kicking him out of their home earlier in the day, walked into the Rowan County, North Carolina, Sheriff's Office to report that his adoptive sister Erica was missing from their family home. Jamie said he hadn't seen Erica since November 2011, a year and a half earlier. The deputies wondered, *Who waits a year and a half to report a sibling missing, especially when that sibling lives in the same house?* Erica would have been fifteen when she was reported missing.

That would be the first in a seemingly unending string of unusual occurrences, deceptions, and downright lies that would play out over the next six years before finally reaching the conclusion with guilty pleas and prison sentences.

Erica Parsons's story eventually became internationally known, with media outlets covering the details from across the world. But it began on a much smaller scale, with local television stations reporting on it from nearby Charlotte, North Carolina, and local newspapers *The Salisbury Post* and *Independent Tribune*. News stories that are covered by local, general assignment reporters can often be told from start to finish in one day, maybe over a few months. Occasionally they take longer, but for a local reporter to cover one particular story for nearly ten years is not typical. That was the case for me with the story of Erica Parsons.

I was a television news reporter with WBTV in Charlotte, North Carolina, a CBS affiliate and the first television station in the Carolinas. WBTV was the only television station that I ever wanted to work for because of its reputation and long standing in the community. I covered the counties north of Charlotte in the North Carolina Piedmont, including Cabarrus, Iredell, Rowan, Stanly, and wherever else they would send me. The story broke after a deputy told me about the unusual report filed about the missing girl, and I drove to the Parsons family home outside of Salisbury, the county seat of Rowan County. The home was a small one-story house that was not particularly well kept, with small cages and signs in the yard advertising "Puppies for Sale."

1: Erica Parsons I

Road work was being done that day, and the road in front of the Parsons's house was reduced to one lane. I parked in the parking lot of a nearby convenience store, where I tried to talk to folks coming in and out, knowing that customers there were likely folks who lived in that area. I spoke with a woman who lived next door to the Parsonses who was stunned—not that Erica had disappeared, but that Erica even existed and lived in the house beside hers. She had never seen Erica Parsons before, but could name every other person who lived there. That neighbor was the first in a very long line of people I would interview about that case over the next ten years.

The adoptive parents of Erica Parsons told law enforcement that Erica wasn't missing and claimed she was with a grandmother named "Nan" in Asheville. They acted like there was nothing to worry about and seemed to just want the story to quietly and quickly disappear. However, investigators, as soon as they started working the case, smelled a rat—or two. If she were safe, why would her brother report her missing?

Even so, Casey and Sandy Parsons could not have predicted how the story would play out in the years after that hot July afternoon in 2013 until 2019, when they pleaded guilty to the torture and murder of Erica Parsons.

But on that day, standing at a convenience store parking lot with my camera and a mic, I had no idea I had only just scratched the surface.

2: Beginnings

My first broadcasting job on WSTP/ WRDX Radio in Salisbury, North Carolina. I was a high school student with a live on-air show each Saturday and Sunday.

As a kid, I never expected that I would be a news reporter and have the chance to inform a large audience about some of the biggest news stories in the world and in my community. I grew up in Salisbury during the 1960s and 1970s. Salisbury is a small city forty miles north of Charlotte. The community is rich in history and its past is treasured to the point that there is a foundation charged with maintaining its history and fighting development that would threaten those tangible reminders of bygone days. The county surrounding it was built on farming and textiles, and Salisbury has a historic section of old homes built in the nineteenth and early twentieth century that are carefully and lovingly preserved.

WBTV is a historic television station with a long tradition of reporting on local news. Folks who grew up in the area loved Channel 3 for local personalities like Fred Kirby. Many local TV stations across the country had their own set of personalities: the news anchors, weather forecasters, horror movie hosts, or any number of characters created to the tastes of their market. Fred Kirby hosted a Sunday afternoon show where he showed the *Little Rascals/Our Gang* comedies, and it was very popular. Fred was a cowboy, always dressed in a red shirt with white fringe, white jeans, boots, and a white cowboy hat. In between the *Little Rascals* shorts, he would play the guitar and sing songs like "Big Rock Candy Mountain" and "Atomic Power." Kirby also appeared in parades and charity events, often riding his horse Calico. More than forty years after the last broadcast, he's still a local icon to many.

Betty Feezor was another reason people watched WBTV. She had a cooking and homemaking show that was very popular. Clyde "Cloudy" McLean was a legendary meteorologist. In the days before computer graphics, Clyde worked from a large board with a black marker, drawing in the highs and lows, the rain, snow, and sunshine. As a CBS affiliate, the station aired Washington Redskins football before the birth of the Carolina Panthers. Channel 3 was the only station my family watched for news.

My first "newscast" was in August of 1974, when, at the age of thirteen, I sat in front of our big console color television and watched President Nixon give his resignation speech. I had been given a small Admiral tape recorder with an external microphone for my birthday that year, and I had that recorder in one hand and the mic in the other. I held it up to the image of Nixon's face on that big console TV set. I was treating it like he was my first exclusive interview. Thankfully, it wouldn't be the last. I still have that cassette.

My first paid broadcasting job was as a deejay on a local radio station in Salisbury when I was sixteen. WSTP was a 1,000-watt AM station playing Top 40 music and included local news and live sports coverage of the area high schools and colleges. WRDX was also in that building, a larger 15,000-watt FM station that played country music. Both stations were owned by Tom Harrell and his ex-wife, Mary Anne Laningham.

One Sunday morning while getting ready for church, I heard an ad on the radio saying WRDX was looking to hire someone to work part time. Along with the country music format, WRDX also had live news and sports and radio staples from the old days, a swap-and-shop-type show that was like classified ads, and local preachers who would pay for fifteen-minute segments to deliver short sermons and devotions. As a big fan of Top 40 and rock, I knew less about country music than I did about nuclear physics, but it was a chance to be on the radio, so I called and made an appointment to inter-view. A week later, I was auditioning in front of a microphone in the station's studio, along with about twelve other young men who had the same dream of local radio stardom. Each one of us got a turn in the production studio reading a package of scripts that included news copy, public service announcements, and commercial copy. I took my time, thinking a deliberate pace that included actually pronouncing each word individually would be better than trying to sound like a late-sixties "boss jock" like the screaming Top 40 disc jockeys in the big markets in New York and California.

At the end of the audition, we were told by the program direc-tor that two would be chosen to fill the weekend hours on WRDX playing music and running commercials for sporting events like NC State football games and NASCAR races. I looked around at the other guys and wondered if maybe, just maybe, I could be one of the two. Two days later, the call came. I did not make the top two, but the program director said I was third, and one of the top two had changed his mind and was no longer interested in the job. My first thought was that one of those two guys was a complete idiot, and that providence had intervened to give me the coveted position.

My initial exuberance was tempered by the training I received at the station. The job wasn't just spinning records and talking into a microphone. I had to keep detailed program logs, check the wire machine for news, even take the readings of the station's transmitter. Doug Rice was one of the established deejays at the station, and would later become the nationally known voice of NASCAR with the Performance Racing Network. He became a close friend and a defining influence on my college life and broadcast career. I enjoyed training with Doug and actually proved to be a quick study to the routine of operating a control board and managing to cue up a 45-rpm single, play commercials from the cart machines, and even talk without sounding like a complete idiot. It's not as easy as it sounds. Well, not always.

My first shift on the air was a Sunday afternoon from one until seven. I was to play current country music dictated by a strict format. The weekly Top 40 on the country charts were all kept in a rack beside the control board. Cabinets containing the oldies and the albums were on the wall behind the board. Conway Twitty, Merle Haggard, and George Jones were producing the hits at the time, as well as Dolly Parton, who had a couple of really big ones. (That's an old radio joke that was frequently heard on country stations to refer to Ms. Parton's buxom figure.) Not really being familiar with the format, and being a devotee of rock and roll, particularly the British invasion, I walked over to the AM station record library and pulled a copy of the Beatles "Get Back." Naturally, I played the record, and watching that black 45 with the bright-green Apple Records label spinning at forty-five revolutions per minute was intoxicating. I never learned to play a musical instrument, so to me, the turntable was my guitar, piano, and drum kit.

It was stupid to think the program director wouldn't be listening to his newest announcer. Within a few minutes, he called me into the control room to let me know that the Beatles could *not*, under any circumstances, fit into the modern country format. He was right, of course, but for the three minutes that "Get Back" was playing, I was on top of the world.

I also spent many hours running the board for those live sports broadcasts. That's where you sit in the booth and play the local commercials during football and basketball broadcasts and NASCAR races. It sounds easy, but you can get bored and your mind wanders, and you can easily miss one of the breaks. I did that a few times and got reprimanded for it. That taught me to pay attention to details and sound cues.

Local sports were a big part of the programming on WSTP and WRDX. The stations carried football games played by the two local college teams, Catawba College and Livingstone College. On days that the two were playing at the same time, we would carry one of the games live, then after it ended, play a tape-delayed broadcast of the other team's game. One Saturday afternoon, I was in a hurry to get off the clock and go out on a date. I was running the board for one of those tape-delayed broadcasts. Not happy with the slow pace of the game, I decided to speed things up. During the commercial breaks, instead of pausing the tape where it was, I fast-forwarded it to the next break. Listeners may have been confused about going into a commercial break with the score in the game something like seven to three, then come out of the sixty-second break with the score now twenty-one to fourteen. I could make a three-and-a-half-hour game be over in about two hours. If anyone ever noticed, they never said anything.

My role at WSTP and WRDX expanded over several years. I began doing color commentary for high school football with Doug. Color commentary is different from play-by-play. Doug would describe what happened with the play on the field, then I would add my own observation about what else happened on that play, how big the crowd was that night, how the weather was, and if the stadium concessions were any good. Color commentary required me to look at more than the play on the field. I also did color for the local American Legion baseball team. The team in Rowan County was like the local New York Yankees; they had a long tradition of winning and even wore the pinstripes. Because there wasn't any minor league ball in the area at the time, the whole county got behind this team and were rewarded with season after season of titles and championships.

The play-by-play man was my friend Howard Platt. Originally from northern Virginia, Howard moved to Salisbury and became a local icon. He was also well-known for his love for the Washington Redskins and UNC Tarheels. We worked together for nearly twenty years broadcasting those American Legion games. Because of the team's success, we traveled to places like Wilmington, North Carolina, and Deland, Florida, for state and national tournaments.

Howard and I developed a fluid working relationship and knew how to interact and have fun on the broadcasts. Also, Howard had another skill set: he had the ability to consume two fully loaded hotdogs within the span of a sixty-second commercial break. If he wasn't going to finish chewing by the time the second spot ended, I'd pick up the broadcast until he was ready, then toss it back to him for the play-by-play. The community really enjoyed the broadcasts, and the games were popular with advertisers.

My radio career continued during my college days at Appalachian State University. ASU is a liberal arts university in Boone, founded in 1899. It is a beautiful campus in the heart of North Carolina's high country, surrounded by the Blue Ridge Mountains, with plenty of skiing, hiking, fishing, and whatever other outdoor sports you'd want to do. Plus, it's the home of many artists and musicians regionally. The radio station there is the college station, WASU. At the time, we called it "91 Rock," and the mascot for it was a guy in a gorilla suit named Rover. I was one of twenty or so disc jockeys, but one of only two or three with actual commercial radio experience. Working at WASU allowed me to play the music that I really loved, and that was a blast. I had the freedom to make a few personal picks that didn't stray too far from the format. If you tuned in during the early eighties, you'd hear songs like "Cars" by Gary Numan, Thomas Dolby's "She Blinded Me With Science," and artists like the Stray Cats, The Clash, The Pretenders, and many more. Local artists like Mike Cross and Bill Agle were also featured. I also got to report news and sports, and even did play-by-play for an App State basketball game. I was horrible on that one-and-done broadcast, but it was a lot of fun.

WASU was low power, I think only 340 watts, but that was more than enough to cover the campus and the surrounding community, and since we were way up in the mountains, few commercial stations from Charlotte or the Greensboro area could be picked up without annoying static.

One of my fellow announcers, frustrated at the lack of power, decided to do something about it. I came into the studio one day to find him standing at the transmitter, holding down the "power increase" switch. I asked him what he was doing, and he told me he was turning it up so that his mother in Charlotte could listen. Luckily, the conviction that I had become impotent due to the sudden power increase on that day later proved false. I turned the power back down and told him to make a tape and mail it to her instead.

My first real brushes with celebrities came while at ASU. The school booked several concerts for homecoming and other big events, and we got some good ones. Some of the performers during my time at App State included the Atlanta Rhythm Section, the Little River Band, and Pablo Cruise. ARS was an established Southern rock band with several big hits, and Pablo Cruise was hot for a couple of years with Top 40 hits like "What You Gonna Do" and "Love Will Find a Way." Then I saw the Nitty Gritty Dirt Band, not on the concert stage, but at a laundromat in Boone. They weren't playing; they had actually pulled the tour bus up and got out to wash their clothes while on the way back from a concert in Tennessee. They were the Dirt Band, cleaning up at a laundromat, and I thought that was too funny.

In recent years, WASU has established an Alumni Takeover Weekend. It's a fundraiser where the old deejays can purchase an hour or two of time and come back to the station and play music from their days on the air. I've taken part in it and absolutely love it. It's a time warp playing those 1980s hits like "Goody Two Shoes" by Adam and the Ants and "Tainted Love" by Soft Cell. The radio station has continued to thrive. While the over-the-air power hasn't increased, it is now accessible online and through an app that allows listeners to tune in from anywhere in the world.

After graduation in 1983, I went back to Salisbury and back to WSTP/WRDX, this time working in the sales department. I married my college sweetheart, Jtan Williams.

Television had not really been at the top of my mind while at ASU. The broadcast journalism major offered there involved classes in stage lighting and other things that I just didn't think could serve me in the future. Instead, I majored in political science and English. When I first met Jtan's father, he asked me what my major was. When I said political science, he replied, "You'll never make any money with that." I didn't have an answer for that, so I just smiled and mumbled something like, "You're probably right."

I settled into this new "executive" job at the radio station. I enjoyed it, as it allowed me to still be on the air occasionally, and I made more money. My responsibility was to sell the ads that you hear on the radio between songs. We called them spots, but Mr. Harrell, the station owner, hated that nickname, always saying that "spots" were things you got on your tie. He preferred the term "commercial announcements." At that time, the stations had a sales staff of about six to eight sales reps. We made a commission on the collections from our sales, and were paid a modest salary to help with expenses. Sales reps could make good money in those days, especially after

WRDX increased power to 100,000 watts and covered Charlotte, Greensboro, and everything in between. It would really have to take something random and out of the blue for me to pursue my early boyhood desire to be on WBTV.

And that's exactly what happened.

WBTV's News Director Ron Miller and Operations Manager Ron Harrington came to visit WSTP one day. I had no idea who they were, but was curious about these two well-dressed men who were meeting with Mr. Harrell. It turns out that Miller and Harrington were in the WSTP studios to talk to the owner about putting a WBTV News bureau in the basement of the radio station. They needed a place to put a studio set with a desk, a background, lights, and a transmitter link, along with equipment for editing videotape. The basement of WSTP was one of the most depressing places on this side of the fiery furnace. Dirt walls and dust-covered piles of promotional albums by artists the station didn't play, like Biz Markie and an Elvis impersonator named Orion. I couldn't believe that a big-time station like WBTV would want something like that for a local news bureau. Tom Harrell couldn't either. As much as he liked the idea of the Charlotte television station paying rent and giving WSTP free publicity, he recommended they look at a seven-story building in downtown Salisbury that had just been renovated and turned into a mix of offices and upscale apartments. The building, originally known as the Grubb Building, later the Wallace Building, and finally as The Plaza, is on the corner of the intersection of Main and Innes streets known as The Square. It's a visible location with a lot of traffic—well . . . a lot for Salisbury.

Miller and Harrington jumped at the idea and started making

the contacts to rent the front office in the historic building. By now I had discovered who these men were and what they wanted. I sent a letter asking if they might need a local yahoo to help them with local contacts and news tips. I figured that could be a golden opportunity for me to get my foot in the WBTV door while still holding down my radio job. To my surprise, they said yes, that they would like to talk with me, and they didn't even use the word *yahoo*.

I didn't know it at the time, but that was the first step toward establishing what would turn out to be a very rewarding career with WBTV.

3: Daddy

My dad introduced me to NASCAR racing. He came in unannounced to pick me up from my fifth-grade class at Overton Elementary School one day to take me to World 600 qualifying at Charlotte Motor Speedway (CMS) about thirty minutes from Salisbury. It was my first time at a racetrack in person, excluding a stop at the North Carolina Motor Speedway in Rockingham at age three, where, according to my mom, I screamed and cried the whole time. On that day in '71, though, I was loving life. I was out of school early and watching that bright Petty-blue Plymouth speed around the track. It was a great day that was followed by coming back on Sunday for the race. That, along with several fishing trips on the coasts of North and South Carolina, are the happy memories I have of Daddy.

My dad, Jake Whisenant, ran a furniture and appliance store in Salisbury. He was originally from Newton-Conover and moved a little over an hour away to Salisbury after he met and married my mom. He served in the Navy in World War II and worked as a Salisbury firefighter before starting the business that he ran for nearly fifty years. He and I were close, and I thought we had a great family dynamic with him, my mom, my sister Pam, and my brother Chris. It took years for me to discover how wrong I was with that assessment.

I only wish that what I thought was true in my home had been reality. We regularly attended Stallings Memorial Baptist Church in Salisbury. Like most folks in Southern Baptist homes, drinking alcohol was not typically something that was done. I had extended family members who were alcoholics, and their example was often used as a deterrence from drinking. Through high school, college, and my adult life, I've never touched it and don't think I've really missed anything by being a teetotaler.

During one of those fishing trips to the coast with my dad when I was in high school, I accidentally found two bottles of vodka in my dad's suitcase. Shocked, I confronted him about it. He seemed embarrassed, but explained that the bottles belonged to my uncle, who "had a problem." Okay, fair enough. That explanation held until I got home and mentioned it to my mother. That's when the dam broke. I learned that my father was an alcoholic and that he'd been drinking secretly for years after he had an issue with painkillers following surgery in the early 1960s. Now it was the early '80s, and he was still hooked. I learned that he kept vodka in a soft-drink cooler in his store and nursed it all day. One day, I poured out the vodka and replaced it with water. He never mentioned it to me.

It seemed I just had to accept that alcoholism was a part of who my dad was, whether I liked it or not.

After Jtan and I were married, we lived in an apartment that wasn't far from my parents' house. Since I was working in sales for the radio station at the time, I could stop in at Daddy's store pretty often to get a cold Cheerwine from a 1950s-era soft drink machine and just sit and talk for a few minutes before I went on a sales call. We would talk for a few minutes, just getting caught up on the day. It was a welcome break for both of us.

After forty-eight years of working full time, my dad decided to retire in 1985 at the age of sixty-five. He held a big retirement sale and closed his store. Then a few months later, much to the disappointment of my mother, he rented another space in the very same block and opened another furniture and appliance store! It seems the idea of being at home all the time just wasn't that appealing, and he was never one to want to travel much. The new store was smaller and had only one other full-time employee, Jack. I still managed to stop by the store often to have a little time with my dad. I didn't stop by there on Tuesday, February 17, 1987, but nearly every day since then, I've wished that I had.

That day was cold, and a freezing rain was falling. Even though there were few people on the road, my dad went to work that morning at eight thirty, just like he had been doing for almost fifty years. I don't know what was going on with him that day, but evidently he was depressed and feeling trapped. Why, I don't know, but that's only one question that will never be answered for me.

In the early afternoon, I got a phone call from my mother saying that something was wrong and asking me to come to her house. I arrived within minutes and found her crying. She told me that something was wrong with Daddy and wanted me to find out what was happening. I called the store, and an employee named Jack answered with the usual, "Good afternoon, City Sales and Rental."

I said, "Jack, this is David. Is anything wrong?"

He replied, "David, your dad is dead. I don't know."

I simply said, "Okay, talk to you later."

I hung up. It took a few hours for me to learn that my sixty-seven-year-old father had taken a .22 pistol from his desk, held the gun to his temple, and pulled the trigger. Jack had been out for lunch, and when he came back, he found Daddy slumped in his chair. The police had called my brother Chris, and he had gone to the store to find him and make arrangements.

I could not understand how this could have happened. Where was the sense in this act? How could the man that played ball with me, took me to church and NASCAR races, taught me some of the best lessons of my life—how could he make the decision to just bail out like this? Why?

This incident was life-changing for me in several ways, and though I had no idea at the time, it would have a profound impact on the kind of news reporter I would become a little more than five years later. At the time of my dad's suicide, the local paper, *The Salisbury Post*, was an afternoon newspaper. It was published daily and had a large circulation. The day after my father died, there was a story on the front page of the paper with the headline "Businessman Shoots Self at His Desk." The story said that my father had put the gun in his mouth and shot himself.

But no, that isn't what happened. Maybe that's a minor error in detail, but it was upsetting. The rest of the story identified my dad and cited a police report as the source of the information. When I later became a reporter, I was always aware of how reporting a story affected those who were involved in it. I know the newspaper had to publish what happened to my dad, but I also felt the paper had the responsibility to get it right.

That principle guided every story I've reported in my thirty-two years. That's not to say that I never made a mistake and never unintentionally upset people, but I did my best to be both accurate and sensitive.

The next few days were a whirlwind of visits and phone calls from family members, friends from church, and many others. Most were welcome and supportive, but others were unintentionally cruel and hurtful. One person wanted to be sure I knew that my daddy was now in Hell because he took his own life. But one of the kindest members of the community, Lester Brown, the owner of a landscaping/lawn and garden company, showed up the next morning at my parents' house with a tractor and a scraper. Without being asked and without a word, he unloaded the tractor and scraped the thin layer of ice from the driveway and the street in front of the house. Most people always say something like, "Let me know if there is anything I can do for you." That's kind and it's appreciated, but Lester Brown's gesture of just showing up and doing that is something I will never forget.

After the funeral, my brother and I worked to close down my dad's store. For several days after his funeral, his customers would come in to see us, to hug, and to cry. It was clear that my dad truly made a positive difference in the community. When he opened his business, it was located in an area of Salisbury known as Chestnut Hill, which was near a large Cone Mills facility that employed hundreds of people. There were dozens of mill houses located on the streets near the store. My dad offered credit purchases to customers with no interest. There was a file cabinet that had hundreds of names on it, and my dad would keep the accounts as customers came in each month to pay their ten- or twenty-dollar payments. Now many of those same customers were coming by to express their sadness and lend their support to me and my brother.

Once the store was shut down, so was any discussion of what had happened—in my family and with our friends. We were upset, of course, but also embarrassed and ashamed. You didn't talk about suicide back then, and the phrase "mental health" was rarely used or understood, especially as it related to suicide. So, I shut up. For years, I didn't talk about what happened to my dad. One time I was asked to give a testimony at church and my mother took me to the side and insisted that I not mention anything about my dad. A few years later, what I can only say was a leading from God prompted me to break the silence about suicide and its effect on those who are left behind.

On the twenty-fifth anniversary of the suicide, in 2012, I took to Facebook to write a long post about what happened and how it had affected me and my family. This is the original post:

Every now and then, I feel the need to write a long form note like this one. Sometimes it's just for fun, or maybe to inform friends about upcoming events. That's not the case with this note. This is something I feel obligated to share with the specific intention of addressing anyone who has seriously considered suicide. Did that last word carry a punch? It certainly did for me when I heard it used to describe what happened on February 17, 1987. It was twenty-five years ago this week.

For reasons that I still don't hold with any certainty, my father, J.R. "Jake" Whisenant, put a .22 pistol to the side of his head and pulled the trigger. He did this while sitting at his desk in the business he had owned and operated on South Main Street in Salisbury for more than forty years.

At the time, I was working at WSTP/WRDX Radio. My mother called and told me that something was wrong and asked me to come home. When I got to my parents' home, I called my dad's store. One of his employees answered in a very normal manner, saying, "City Sales and Rental, can I help you?" I told him who it was and asked if everything was okay. His reply still runs through my mind frequently. He said, "David, your dad's dead. I don't know." I thanked him and hung up.

So there it is, the reason I wanted to post this note. It's to say to anyone who has ever considered suicide that it should be immediately ruled out as a viable option. What may appear to be an alluring answer and immediate exit from the troubles of the day is, in reality, a horror that continually renews itself for those who are left behind. I'm a survivor, and that's tougher than you may think. When someone commits this act, I'm convinced they are not giving any thought to what will happen to loved ones. It certainly puts an end to their trouble, but it opens up difficulties and challenges that last for years, at least for twenty-five.

What are you left with after a suicide? Along with the emotional toll, there's the constant questioning, the hurt of physical loss; then there are the practical issues of dealing with financial matters, answering unintentionally insensitive and religiously flawed questions, even having to do extraordinarily painful things like packing up clothes and other personal items.

To say time heals all wounds doesn't entirely apply to suicide. Certainly, distance from that day dims some of the raw memories, but as recently as this past Sunday, a fresh wound was opened in a place where it would have been least expected, leading me to react in a hostile and immature fashion that is inconsistent with my nature.

Suicide wrings the mental health out of those who are left behind. I'm convinced that my father's suicide led, at least in part, to my brother's alcoholism, which in turn led to his throat cancer and eventual death at an early age. Both were alcoholics. I've abstained from alcohol my entire life and would gladly offer that as good advice, but that's a moral crusade for another day.

To make it simple: don't do it. Don't consider it. My faith in God is what sustains me in troubled times. Let me encourage you to seek that faith, and if you're comfortable with it, seek professional counseling. If you truly love your family and your friends, you will not want them to go through what survivors of suicide have to face. Don't do it. Don't do it. Don't do it. Think of me as the guy waving his arms to try and stop you before you drive around the blind curve and off the cliff. That's all I can say. Don't do it.

That phrase, "Don't do it," became my mantra on this issue. The note had traction and was read and shared thousands of times over. Keith Larson, a very popular talk show host on WBT Radio in Charlotte, graciously invited me to speak on his show. *The Salisbury Post* printed the Facebook post. WBTV also put together a story that anchors Molly Grantham and Jamie Boll promoted. It was overwhelming for me to realize what an impact I could have and how many people I could reach with this message.

3: Daddy

I've continued to tell my father's story on TV and social media. Every few years, I record a new video and post it on YouTube. I do feel like God has given me the responsibility to talk about the suicide based on my experiences with it. It's very hard to do, and sometimes I go through phases of just not wanting to talk about it or deal with it at all, but those are things I have to work through. I didn't seek professional counseling until an event I observed on the job much later compelled me to do so. I have had counseling since that time, and it's almost always tied back to issues I have because of my dad's suicide.

Over the last few years, I've taken part in an initiative created by the United Way in Rowan County. It's called Into the Light, and it deals with suicide and mental health. People gather early on a Saturday morning and begin walking around the track that circles the football field at Catawba College. As we walk, the sun rises over the visitor grandstand, graphically showing how we have walked from the predawn darkness into the light of the sun, while also bringing suicide and mental health "into the light." Survivors of suicide attempts often express regret for trying to take their lives. This walk symbolically shows how everything can change if you just give it a few minutes more, you can move from total darkness into the light. The event draws a couple hundred people each year. People share their experiences with suicide, and then I usually speak to offer a challenge about seeking help. I truly hate taking part in the event because it magnifies the pain and makes it top of mind again, but I wouldn't be anywhere else. It's something that I think is so important and I'll support it any way I can.

Once more thing: when it comes to suicide, don't do it.

4: Stringer Life

Powering up my first TV camera in the spring of 1992.

WHILE STILL WORKING AT THE RADIO STATION, I started my television career in the spring of 1991 at the bottom of the ladder as a stringer. That's someone who works freelance, running out and shooting spot news like car wrecks, crime scenes, parades, festivals, and house fires. I didn't have a professional camera, so Ron Harrington had me come to WBTV and learn how to use a Sony three-quarter-inch camera that was connected to a tape deck. The camera was cool, but the tape deck that you had to carry with it wasn't. It was roughly the size and thickness of a door from a 1963 Lincoln Continental and weighed as much as a cinder block dog house. To this day, my body has a distinct lean to the right from carrying this gear.

Inside the new bureau WBTV set up in Salisbury, they'd placed videotape decks and a small transmitter that sent a signal to the roof, which then transmitted to Young Mountain, 1,003 feet above Cleveland, North Carolina, and then on to WBTV. My responsibility was to record video of whatever the event was, then return to the bureau, call an engineer, and feed the video back to Charlotte. I didn't know how to edit tape, so I just sent the raw video, which could be between five and thirty minutes long. An editor at the station would take my video and reduce it down to a manageable twenty to thirty seconds and get it on the air during the next scheduled newscast.

At first, I didn't write scripts that were read with the video. This was before the internet and email. I provided just the facts over the phone, and a producer would write the script, usually running it by me to make sure it was accurate before putting it on air.

My first assignment came just three days after I picked up all the gear from Charlotte. The woman working the assignment desk in the Charlotte newsroom took a call that there was a riot at a bar in downtown Salisbury. She wanted me to shoot some video, maybe interview some people, and talk to the police—all on a Saturday night. I wanted this assignment like a marathon runner wants wingtips. *Me, go to a riot at a bar? With a camera?* That was crazy talk! Then my loving wife reminded me that it was my dream to work for WBTV, and I'd said I would do whatever I could to help out and get started. So I drove to the bar.

There was no riot. It had happened the night before, and several people had been arrested. There was talk of trouble again that night, so there were several police officers in the area. When I drove up, I parked about a block from the bar. I didn't see anything that looked like a riot, or even a mild disagreement, but I dutifully hopped out, put the camera on the same tripod that must have been used to film the Normandy invasion, and began rolling off the first frames of video. I shot about eight minutes' worth, an eternity in local television news. I went to the bureau and fed the video to the station. The video ran the next day on the noon news, then again at six. I was amazed to see how good it looked once it was in the capable hands of an editor.

I was on my way, flush with the excitement of having completed my first assignment and not screwing it up.

As a stringer, I was paid on a per story basis. Each story I shot was worth fifty dollars, plus mileage. If I shot enough for a reporter to create a full story, or a "package," the price went up to sixty dollars. I also made twelve dollars for each tip I called in to the station. A typical month was October 1994. I did stories ranging from a Tennessee fugitive caught in North Carolina to a price dispute at the county fair, a sex offender's arrest, a campaign to educate teens on the dangers of drunk driving, and four high school football games for our very popular *Football Friday Night* show. That month's work was worth a total of $2,822.50.

After two years as a stringer, I began to shoot stories in which I acted as the reporter. That isn't something most stringers would do. They would be happy being a stringer and didn't want to take the extra time to shoot and edit the additional video, but I knew that I wanted to become a reporter. I would finish shooting whatever the story was, then put the camera on the tripod, run around to the other side, and present the story as if I were reporting it with a cameraman on the other side. When I sent in the stories without the reporting that the station wanted, I would also include these stories with my reporting, because they represented a complete version of the story with video, interviews, and me—all edited into a piece that usually ran a minute and a half.

After a while, either because the news director thought my work was brilliant, or they really got tired of seeing these mock-up stories, they asked me to actually become a reporter and produce my own stories for air.

My first package where I appeared on the air was shot in April 1994. The story was about Barber-Scotia College in Concord, North Carolina. The school was having to send students home less than a month before they graduated because they had not paid their tuition. I interviewed a representative from the school and then found a couple of students carrying their belongings out to their cars for the trip home. That night, I sat with my family around the television in the living room, getting so nervous when legendary WBTV anchorman Bob Inman read my name as he introduced my story. Even though the story was recorded and had been approved, I was convinced that something would go wrong. But it didn't, and as it turned out, it was a good start. From that day on, I considered myself a bona fide television news reporter. I had the chance to learn what stories interested the station and which ones caused them to think I was a helpless rube.

Stringer life continued for about two years before I officially became a full-time WBTV reporter. I was shooting so many stories that the station decided they would be better off making me a full-time reporter. It meant a pay cut to start with, but I knew it was a better opportunity. I did continue to do the *Football Friday Night* high school football show for several more years on the radio, though.

Being a stringer was a wonderful education that prepared me

to be a reporter/photographer. I was able to build relationships and learn many basic rules about working around crime, accident, and disaster scenes, and how to find the best places to get the best shots. I would have been much less of a reporter without that time spent on the eyepiece side of the camera. I also got to meet some of the public service professionals who would go on to define and shape my career.

5: East Spencer Fire

Reporting on personal tragedies in the community is a big part of a reporter's job. Those stories can be profound, and the kind of story that justifies what many in the media genuinely try to do each time we stand in front of a camera or sit in front of a keyboard. Reporters have to be sensitive to the individuals involved, but also accurate in how the story is reported.

It was a lazy Sunday afternoon in February 1995, and I was still technically a stringer for WBTV, being paid on a per story basis. That was my motivation for often listening to a police and fire emergency scanner. I was at home after church, eating a hearty lunch, with the scanner on in the background, hoping that if something happened, I could run out and shoot it and pocket a quick seventy-five dollars. Sure enough, I heard a dispatch sent out to the East Spencer Fire Department that there was smoke in one area of the town.

East Spencer is a small community of around 1,400 people that borders Salisbury in Rowan County. The town grew up in the shadow of the huge Southern Railway repair facility that used to be in the town of Spencer, just over the railroad tracks. East Spencer is a predominantly African-American community that is home to a big grocery chain warehouse and a large brick manufacturing plant. Not being very large, the town at that time did not have paid firefighters, but relied on volunteers.

When I heard that dispatch, I knew that I'd better get my camera and head that way. The East Spencer Fire Department had numerous problems when it came to fighting fires because their equipment was old and there weren't many volunteers. Often, it took the volunteers a long time to leave their homes or jobs, get to the station to get the fire trucks, and then get to the fire scene. Just a month before, I arrived at a fire scene before the fire department and shot video of a police officer grabbing a garden hose and trying to put out the flames while waiting on the firefighters.

My hunch proved to be correct. I arrived at the house before the East Spencer firefighters. I lived nine miles away, and the fire department was located just three blocks from the burning house. A small white wooden frame house was billowing smoke from a screened porch on the back. It didn't look that serious. A few neighbors were standing around, and one told me that the family who lived in the house was still at church. Within a few minutes, the first fire truck arrived, and the firefighters set about pulling hose and finding the nearest hydrant. By then, the smoke was getting thicker and darker, and the fire was starting to spread quickly. The firefighters put water on it, but this only made it angrier and more intense. Before long, the house was engulfed in smoke, and flames were tearing a ragged hole through the thin gray shingles on the roof.

I was getting every image on my camera: the spreading flames, the smoke, the futility of the firefighter's actions, the bewildered expressions on the faces of neighbors, who—like me—thought the fire would have at least been under control by this point. But it burned on.

Then a four-door car, loaded with a woman and several children, came down the narrow street. It came as far as it could before having to stop for the fire trucks that were blocking the road. A woman got out and moved closer in slow motion. She was staring intently at the burning house. Her eyes had that look of denial, like whatever it was they were seeing couldn't be what's really happening. Lelia Geter was watching her home go up in smoke, and it didn't appear that anybody could do anything to stop it.

I couldn't shoot any more video. I know I should have gotten a shot of Lelia walking toward the house, of the neighbors rushing to help her and hold her back, but I just couldn't do it. I took my camera off the tripod and just waited. A family of seven had just lost everything they owned, including a dog, and I had it all on a three-quarter-inch tape in my camera.

Eventually the fire was extinguished, more from the fact that there was nothing left to burn than from the efforts of firefighters. I went back to the bureau and edited: forty-five seconds of pictures and sound for our six and eleven p.m. news. The next day, the station wanted to do a follow-up story. They sent a veteran reporter named Mike Matthews. I admired his work and still think he's one of the best television journalist storytellers I've ever seen. Matthews and a Charlotte photographer and I went back to that house to find Lelia Geter and two of her boys, eight-year-old Wraymel and ten-year-old Fernando, walking through the charred remains of what had been their home. They were gracious enough to allow us to walk with them, videotaping the experience and recording their words.

"That used to be my bedroom," said Wraymel. "That was a new bed."

Later, Fernando found the frame of the bike he had gotten for

Christmas less than two months earlier. Lelia talked about "starting from the bottom again" and how in surveying the damage, her only thought was, "I don't see nothing."

Mike did a masterful job in writing and telling the story. Several years earlier, Mike, too, had lost most of his possessions in a fire, so he wrote with an empathy that few could duplicate. The photographer used my video of the fire, along with the interviews from the next day, to create a compelling story. As it turned out, that story was so powerful, it produced something I had not yet experienced in my career: action.

The emotion of the story had touched our viewers, which produced an overwhelming response. People from all across our viewing area began calling the TV station and asking how they could help, wanting to give money, clothes, anything at all to help this family. A man in Hickory told them they could live in a house he owned rent-free until they got on their feet. A Walmart manager donated bikes; a furniture store manager offered new furniture; and they had enough donated clothes to outfit the entire family for the next three decades. Cash came pouring into a fund established by the local Red Cross, and there were enough offers of free puppies to fill a kennel.

That's when the impact of my job really hit me for the first time: what I was doing could actually be used for good and could help improve lives. I guess I'd always known that was true, but seeing this immediate public response firsthand really showed me that there was something honorable and decent that came from working in the media. Being a reporter doesn't always have to be about exploiting people at their lowest point. Yes, I still had to shoot the fire, and I still had to be that intrusive reporter standing there while tragedy unfolded, but that's what created the context in which I could tell this story. The piece Mike Matthews did would not have had the impact without my video of flames and smoke destroying the house. Those were the images, coupled with the emotions of Lelia, Wraymel, and Fernando Geter, that brought about change and inspired perfect strangers to take action on their behalf. This epiphany forever changed the way I looked at my job and the responsibility the media has to the public to let them know what's happening to people in our community.

Two months later, I talked to Lelia Geter again. The station wanted me to do a follow-up story to see how the family had fared. "We're doing great," Lelia told me. "I don't know what I would do to say thank you for what they did, because they really didn't have to do that, but they went from their hearts and gave us this stuff, and God knows I am truly thankful, Lord, I'm thankful."

The impact of that story also went in another positive direction. The East Spencer Fire Department became determined to improve how they did their jobs. The fire chief in neighboring Salisbury took my raw video and conducted classes for the East Spencer volunteers. Knowing that my video was being used to train firefighters was gratifying.

This story can still make tears well up in my eyes when I retell it. It also confirmed for me the necessity of putting myself in uncomfortable and awkward moments for my role as a journalist. When the family came home from church to find a burning shell of what had been their home, I felt terrible that I was standing there shooting video. It wasn't until a couple of days later that I realized how important my presence had been for that family to get relief and support.

There have been more moments like that throughout my career, where I stood by the road near a fatal crash or outside a home where a crime had just occurred. I reminded myself that I have a job to do and that what I'm doing in those moments can be valuable in the days that follow. Even in cases where the family members and friends of victims scream and shout and hurl insults at me while I'm there behind a camera, they would often have a change of heart if we were able to talk later and perhaps do a follow-up story. This happens when they come to realize—as in the case of a missing person or an unsolved crime—the value of keeping a story alive and the hope of bringing about a resolution.

6: Cops

A typical crime scene with a patrol car, yellow police tape, and evidence markers on the street to indicate where spent bullets were found.

POLICE OFFICERS, DEPUTIES, AND HIGHWAY PATROL troopers are the people television reporters spend a lot of time with while pursuing stories. The relationship can be good or tense. I tend to blame other members of the media when I run into those awkward situations. It usually comes about when a reporter uses information that is considered off the record or does something to betray a source or harm an investigation for the sake of a story. I've had to work hard to repair some damaged relationships left behind by members of the media who put their story before the public good.

I started making beat calls to the sheriff of Rowan County to catch up on any news that I might be able to pitch to WBTV. Every morning I went to the sheriff's office and police department to speak in person with an investigator. I would ask about any overnight crime or anything they might be working on. Those in-person visits were valuable in building trust in our relationships, and they allowed me to stay on top of anything that was happening.

Bob Martin was in his sixties at the time and had been elected sheriff of Rowan County after he retired from a long and colorful career with the Bureau of Alcohol, Tobacco, and Firearms. Martin had spent years chasing moonshiners in the hills of North Carolina, including Junior Johnson, who later became a famous NASCAR driver and team owner.

Martin had one particularly troublesome encounter with a moonshiner who took a shot at him with a handgun. Martin and another agent were waiting at the man's still in Davidson County. They knew he would come home soon, and they wanted to arrest him for several charges related to moonshining. What they didn't know is that twenty-nine-year-old James Shirley had a shotgun and was deeply determined not to be captured. "I was going to tackle him," Martin told me several years later. "He turned and fired. It knocked my finger off; my thumb was pushed back." Martin fell to the ground in pain; the man grabbed Martin's .38, stood over him, and squeezed the trigger. It should have been a fatal shot. "I was trying my best to talk him out of shooting and he was trying his best to shoot me," said Martin. Thankfully, the gun didn't fire. It had been broken by the blast from Shirley's shotgun. Shirley ran away and then committed suicide when agents approached him.

Before I ever met the sheriff, I heard several stories about him, including a short version of that moonshiner encounter. The morning that I went to his office for the first time, I was met by one of the other high-ranking deputies. He wanted to talk to me before I met the sheriff. He said it was a friendly way of "getting me ready." I appreciated that he was taking the time to help me. I sat across from the deputy at his desk while he explained to me about the sheriff being in that altercation that had left him without a thumb. "The miracle," he said, "was that the doctors were able to fix Bob's thumb by removing his big toe and placing it where the thumb used to be." Armed with this amazing bit of delightful information, I walked into his office and shook his hand. That hand. My eyes were drawn to the toe/thumb. It looked deformed—a plump, pink thumb with a nail that looked more like an eagle talon right in the middle.

After saying hello, I spoke about how interesting it was that the doctors could do something so amazing: imagine, a big toe replacing a thumb!

There are moments in life when you wish you could disappear into thin air. Moments when you would give anything to be able to slap your hands on your forearms, blink tightly like a genie, hear a sound effect, and find yourself on a lush island, a mountaintop, or inside a dumpster—just anywhere else. This power, unfortunately, eluded me at that moment. Sheriff Martin developed a puzzled look on his face, looked right at the toe/thumb, gazed at me and said, "Whisenant, what the hell are you talking about? This isn't my toe." Before I could think of anything to say, the laughter coming from down the hall filled in the awkward silence. At once, he understood that I had been the victim of a prank. He still had a hard time believing I fell for it.

I ended up working pretty closely with Sheriff Martin over the years and always admired his professionalism, his sense of humor, and his thumb.

There are times when the law enforcement official becomes

bigger than life, and that always makes for interesting reporting. In my case, it was a tall man with salt-and-pepper hair and an ego as large as the overgrown baseball bat he liked to carry with him: former Davidson County Sheriff Gerald Hege. He wore all black and drove a black Chevrolet Impala SS with a giant silver decal of a black widow spider on the hood. Called the "spider car," it had actually been tuned up by NASCAR team owner Richard Childress, who was a friend of Hege's. Davidson County was not part of the area covered by WBTV, but Hege had created such a reputation that my news director thought it would be fun to profile him in a story. He was right.

By this time in my career, I was able to occasionally have a photographer assigned to help me with stories. On longer form personality stories like this, the station wants the reporter to be able to concentrate on the subject and not be concerned with camera angles. My photographer that day was George Williams. George was an experienced and very capable news videographer who was close to retirement. He helped me learn that even a news camera is capable of creating art. There are elements that news photographers can look for to help tell a story: sunsets, mountain views, clouds, even neighborhoods with manicured lawns can be shot in such a way that they look compelling and can create a better story. George and I worked well together, and he was looking forward to this assignment. We had the same sense for what video we wanted and how many interviews were needed to put together a full story. When we arrived, Sheriff Hege greeted us enthusiastically and led us into his office.

Hege's office was designed to look like a military encampment. There were weapons all around, camouflage netting, boxes of ammo, and one feature you don't normally find in a war zone: television lights. Hege had the lights installed because he was getting a lot of attention from media outlets across the country, so I guess it really wasn't too outrageous. Hege had actual TV lights wired into the ceiling, pointing at him. Of course, it was great for George and me since the lights were already in place and properly balanced. We did a short interview there in what he called "the bunker." We laid out what we wanted for the story, and Hege was only too happy to oblige. Our next step was to walk out to the spider car and take a short ride with him to the firing range.

We got in the car, me in the front and George in the back so that he could get some shots of Hege and me talking in the car. Hege fired up the Chevy, and the roar of the powerful engine was completely drowned out by the ear-splitting volume of "Bad to the Bone" by George Thorogood. It was obvious that Hege had planned that by cueing up the CD to come on with that song the moment the engine started. I'm not even sure if the song had reached the vocal yet when the normally mild-mannered George yelled, "Please turn that down!"

Hege replied, "What?"

George said, "Turn it down!"

Hege made the adjustment, George shook his head and mumbled something I didn't quite understand, and we were off.

Now there were stories about Hege flagrantly violating traffic laws in Davidson County. I knew he wouldn't do anything like that with a news reporter and a photographer in the car. Or so I thought. But at one point on Highway 8 we were doing 100 miles an hour. I asked the sheriff why we were doing that and if we might back it off a bit. His reply was that he just wanted to show us what that souped-up Chevy could do.

At the firing range came more displays of bravado. Sheriff Hege was shooting at stuff with handguns, shotguns, machine guns, an endless barrage of "pow pow pow, rat-a-tat-tat, yippee yippee hooah." Okay, I got it. At the end of the day, I had an autographed poster of Hege and a CD with him on the cover. I don't think he sang—I never listened to it. I think it was a tribute song by Billy Wayne Ray Bob Wayne or some other budding country star. It was just the kind of thing that would end up in the WSTP basement, collecting dust beside Biz Markie.

George and I then drove back in a much quieter car, at a more sensible speed, to get to work.

The story we did really turned out well, though. George managed to even use the snippet of "Bad to the Bone" to set the mood. Hege came off looking exactly like he was—a sheriff with a huge ego—who, in spite of it all, had some qualities that made you feel like the bad guys wouldn't want to face him. Hege later claimed national fame when he painted the cells in the Davidson County jail pink with images of sad crying teddy bears. He also made the inmates wear pink-and-white-striped jumpsuits instead of the standard orange. I have to admit, seeing those tough scoundrels walking around doing community service in pink-and-white jumpsuits was hilarious. Hege also had a show on national television airing on Court TV called *Inside Cell Block F* that he hosted from that very jail. It consisted of him interviewing inmates in his jail, talking about their lives and the circumstances that put them behind bars. There was also a hefty dose of his black-and-white, no-nonsense advice.

Of course, all of this was too good to be true; Hege and his department were caught up in a scandal involving drugs and evidence, and in September 2003, Hege was suspended from office after he was charged with embezzlement, obtaining property by false pretenses, and other charges. He eventually took a plea agreement in the case and the charges were expunged. I don't know where he is now. He did recently make an unsuccessful bid to win back the office of sheriff. I learned over the years, that for every macho swaggering Buford Pusser/Walking Tall type in law enforcement, there are at least ten cops who don't fit that mold.

Pusser was the no-nonsense sheriff of McNairy County, Tennessee, from 1964 to 1970. He gained legendary status for taking on such vices as gambling, prostitution, and moonshining. Pusser was the subject of several movies and portrayed by Dwayne "The Rock" Johnson in the latest *Walking Tall* film in 2004.

The law enforcement officers I dealt with didn't really fit that mold. They are the hard-working detectives, officers, deputies, and administrators who make up that "thin blue line" that separates chaos from civilization. If you cover local news, you will have a lot of interactions with law enforcement, and if you treat them with respect, you will not only have the peace of mind that comes from knowing you are doing the right thing and reporting with ethics, you will also benefit by having a better and more accurate story.

In my time in Salisbury, I've watched with admiration as Black police officers in riot gear protected marchers and speakers at a Ku Klux Klan rally on the steps of the courthouse. As police officers, it is their duty to protect citizens, even when they may hate them and are disgusted with what they are shouting into a megaphone just a few feet away. While one man clad in purple robes shouted racial slurs at the crowd and continually used racial epithets and profanity to describe Dr. Martin Luther King Jr., these officers stood silently, watching for any threat to this redneck orator. Later, during an interview, the officers told me they just tried to tune out the noise and focus on doing their jobs.

One of the only times I was really frightened on the job was in the hours following a shootout in East Spencer. One night in October of 1997, two East Spencer officers were delivering warrants to a small house down a side street off one of the main roads. As they approached the house, they were ambushed by a man named Movell Daniels. His mugshot showed a wild-eyed, maniacal face. As officers approached the house, he fired on them, striking Officer Robert Clement twice. Clement lay on the front porch of the house, unable to move. Other officers risked their own lives to move in, using their police cruiser as a shield to drive up to the front porch so that they could pull Clement to safety.

I'd gotten a tip about the shooting. I was on my way to the scene when I called the station and told them to send me some help, as I knew this was going to be a big story and we would need more than one camera and the ability to go live from as close to the house as we would be allowed. I pulled into a grocery store parking lot about three blocks from the house and parked beside a trooper with the North Carolina State Highway Patrol. He and I were both at the back of our cars; he was getting his shotgun and bulletproof vest, while I was grabbing my camera, tripod, and lights. Suddenly, we heard loud gunfire, five or six shots. I flinched, ducked down to the ground, and then noticed something extraordinary. The trooper was still standing upright, calmly putting on his vest. I thought it was incredible, and when I asked him why he hadn't ducked too, he explained that from the sound of the gunfire, he knew it really wasn't a threat to us. I had never seen that kind of cool before. After a while, we were repositioned on the other side of the crime scene. I had a decent view of the front porch through my zoom lens. I was standing in a staging area where the SWAT team was preparing to make an entry. I was reporting live, standing right beside them as they loaded up weapons and mapped out their plan of attack.

As it turned out, that entry was never made; a different plan was preferred. Officers waited all through the night, keeping a silent vigil with guns trained on that house from every angle. Night turned to morning, still with no resolution. We knew that Officer Clement and another officer who had been shot were at the hospital, but we didn't know anything about the shooter, Movell Daniels. No one had seen any movement inside the house or heard a sound since the actual shooting. Sometime around midmorning, the SBI sent a robot into the house equipped with a camera. It promptly got hung up on a rug and fell over on its side. Even so, something—and to this day I'm not sure what it was—convinced lawmen that they should go into the house. When they did, they found Daniels already dead from a self-inflicted gunshot wound. He had probably been dead for hours.

Thankfully Robert "Bert" Clement survived the shooting, though one of the two bullets that hit him struck his spine, leaving him unable to use his right leg and right hand. I later did several stories with him that chronicled his recovery. I interviewed him in his hospital bed in Winston-Salem, then later as he underwent painful rehabilitation. One particularly enjoyable story was on how

Bert and his therapist worked on regaining his mobility in a swimming pool. In the water, Bert could walk and move freely. He really enjoyed it and was making progress. He joked around, talked about being a police officer again, and loved to show me all the Oakland Raiders merchandise he had gotten since the shooting. He did one interview from the hospital bed wearing a Raiders cap.

Bert's progress continued for more than a year, and then tragedy struck again. Bert was having surgery to reroute a muscle to his foot, but a blood clot broke loose and went to his heart and lung. He suffered brain damage and died a few days later.

I'll never forget that funeral. I wanted to capture it all on camera and edit it into a moving tribute to a fallen hero: the bagpipes playing "Amazing Grace," the tears of police officers standing at attention in full uniform under a blazing hot sun in a rural church cemetery, Bert's wife Lunda, always strong, always faithful. She gave me an interview after the service was complete, and I still appreciate that. It gave me some context and a point of view for the story I had to tell that night, and it made it their story, Bert and Lunda's, not mine, and those are always better.

Several years later, WBTV would again call on me to cover a police funeral. This time for two Charlotte-Mecklenburg officers killed in the line of duty. I had never met Sean Clark or Jeff Shelton. They were killed in March 2007, responding to a call. I was called in that night to go to the hospital where the officers had been taken. I worked through the night, also covering the police chief's press conference around five the next morning.

The station had me cover the officers' funeral, or more precisely, the procession from the church to the gravesite. I did that from

Sky 3, our news helicopter. WBTV was the first Charlotte station to have a news helicopter, and I always enjoyed when I got to ride in it for a story. This was one of the most memorable sights I'd ever witnessed. The procession took about forty-five minutes, moving slowly through the heart of Charlotte. On every street, every sidewalk, every intersection were throngs of people. Many held flags or signs, many more held their hands over their hearts. It was one of the most emotional displays of sympathy I have ever seen. At a construction site, a group of Hispanic workers stopped their work and stood together, hard hats over their hearts. At other spots I saw scout troops, church groups, individuals, all waiting for hours for those few minutes when the cars would pass by. The procession itself featured hundreds of cars from CMPD, but also patrol cars from police, sheriffs' departments, and state and federal agencies from all across the county.

Over the years, I covered several more processions honoring the lives of law enforcement officers who died in the line of duty. From deputies in Watauga County to police officers in Charlotte and several other municipalities, the strains of the bagpipes playing "Amazing Grace" became a hauntingly familiar and mournful sound. This filled me again with a sense of responsibility to tell an accurate story describing what I had seen, and I had to do it professionally, not in a maudlin way trying to evoke some emotional reaction. I always prayed about how I wanted to present these stories with the right balance of truth and tribute. I reflected in the days following the Clark and Shelton story that, while it may have been the most moving display I had ever seen, I hoped I would not have to witness anything like that again.

7: The Goat Boys

I'M OFTEN ASKED MY FAVORITE STORIES FROM my career in television. That's a difficult task, simply because of the number of stories I did during any given year. If you consider that I was a reporter for more than thirty years, covering at least one story per day, five days a week, that comes up to 755,098,758,987 stories. Roughly the size and scope of the federal stimulus bailout program or the national debt. There is one story, though, that rises from the mists of my mind, and brings a chuckle to me and (hopefully) to anyone who hears it.

It was July 5, 1995, and the story was about two young men whom I refer to as "the goat boys." They don't have cloven hooves or bodies like those freaky centaurs. They were just two normal teenagers living in a very rural part of Iredell County, about thirty miles west of Charlotte. Trae Whitlow and Donnie Minter were good friends and needed summer jobs. While some boys sought employment as lifeguards, doing yard work, or babysitting, Trae and Donnie rented out goats under the company name (non-LLC and registered, I assure you) "Rent A Goat." A schoolteacher had made the suggestion and Grandpa Marvin helped the boys get started. I don't know whose grandpa Marvin actually was, but it didn't seem that important. I drove to the small house off Highway 21 and met the boys and their goats. The idea was that people could rent these goats from these teens to eat their grass and weeds. "Like honeysuckles, poison oak, poison ivy, if you're allergic to that, they'll go right through it," said Donnie, sounding like budding pitchman Billy Mays (who famously said, "But wait, there's more!").

I knew I was going to have fun with this story. The boys were funny, the goats were entertaining and energetic, and it had all the elements of some of the finest cheese I could produce. When I shot my stand-up, which is the part of the story where the reporter is on camera saying something important and groundbreaking, here's what I said: "The best summer job I had wasn't so sweet. I had a lemonade stand. All the profits were sour, and I ended up with sticky fingers. These guys have done their homework. They studied the community and found that a goat rental service was something that was baaa-dly needed here." *Groan.*

Now these boys and their entourage were excited for the big TV station from Charlotte to be telling their story, so naturally there was a bit of showing off to be done. Donnie and Trae wanted me to witness their prowess at riding the goats. The boys took turns jumping on the backs of the unwilling goats and attempting to hang on for the required eight seconds of rodeo time. That's about as long as they could do it. The goats, who evidently are pretty smart, knew just what to do to get these boys off their backs: they ran right into a thicket of trees with the lowest branches at just the right height to knock their passengers off and onto their behinds.

On and on it went, jumping on goats, goats running, boys falling, everybody laughing. I must have shot ten minutes of this exercise from every angle. If the camera hadn't been so big and heavy back then, I think I would have duct taped it to the goat for a better vantage point.

After several hours, I made my way back to Salisbury to put this story together, excited at the possibilities. I labored over the script, trying to be both funny and informative about the benefits of goat rental. And I used a good deal of the video of the goats throwing the boys on the ground.

At the time, I had to get every script approved by a producer before I started editing. The script passed approval, but one of the producers watched the story as I fed it in and was horrified at the video of the boys trying to ride the goats. She told me we couldn't use that video because it was animal cruelty. Animal cruelty? Are you kidding? The animals were the clear winners in this exchange, so if anything, I felt it was child abuse. Even so, the word of the producer ruled the day, so I had to start over with a new script and without the best video I had. The story still turned out pretty well, and I got a lot of comments on it. I don't know how successful the boys' goat enterprise was that summer. They were charging a dollar a day per goat, so I figure at best they pocketed around $150 for the summer. Considering the low overhead of not having to feed and house the goats, that's really not baaaaaad.

8: Katrina

The miserable but necessary duty of getting out in the elements to report on hurricanes and other forms of severe weather. This is me covering Hurricane Dorian near Myrtle Beach, South Carolina, in September 2019.

YOU'VE SEEN TV REPORTERS COVERING HURRICANES, RIGHT? Where we risk our lives standing outside to tell people not to stand outside? We drive around in a storm to tell people not to drive around. This is when you see reporters getting blown off of their feet, tied to power poles, or any number of questionable behaviors to try to show viewers how truly bad the storm is. Some reporters love covering hurricanes. They are the first to put their hand up when a tropical depression develops and the news director asks if anyone wants to volunteer to head to the coast.

Not me.

I've covered a few hurricanes off the coast of North and South Carolina. It's not my thing, but when asked to go, I did my best while trying to stay alive. Then came Katrina on August 29, 2005.

Hurricane Katrina was one of the biggest natural disasters ever

"

to hit the United States. The Government Accounting Office, citing the National Oceanic and Atmospheric Administration, estimated the cost of damage caused by Katrina to be over $170 billion, and 1,833 people died as a result of Katrina. To say it was an epic event is quite the understatement.

The storm hit pretty close to home for my family. My wife's sister Judy and her husband Brian lived in Waveland, Mississippi, a small town near other small towns with names like Bay St. Louis, Godeau, and Pearlington. Some of those names would be well known in the days following Katrina. Bryan and Judy's house was a half mile from the coast, and after the storm, it was oceanfront.

Before Katrina, Jtan, our son Kyle, and I had spent a couple of summer vacations with Brian and Judy at their house. We loved the hot weather, the Catholic church's seafood festival, and going to buy delicious Gulf shrimp right off the boats. My sister-in-law would take us down all kinds of rural back roads to see people who lived on small houseboats and on mobile homes erected on pilings eight to ten feet above the ground. It never occurred to them that eight feet wouldn't be high enough to protect them from this monster storm.

The day after Katrina hit, I offered to go to the Gulf Coast and put together a few stories on the damage and how people were coping. The news director at WBTV loved the idea, especially since I volunteered to go alone. That was the first of many mistakes I made.

I left the next morning in a brand new "live" truck. That's a large van that television stations use to broadcast to the station via a microwave transmitter. You can spot a live truck by the tall mast on the back that can rise to a height of sixty feet or better. In this case, I wasn't taking the truck to use the microwave transmitter, but to have all the editing equipment set up in the back of the truck. With one of those trucks, you have everything you need to do a complete news story, including a live shot. My idea was to go to the Waveland area and shoot several stories, then edit them down and go to Atlanta to a dish farm and feed them back to Charlotte through a satellite uplink.

It all sounded so fun and easy.

Driving through Georgia and approaching Atlanta, I had the first inkling that maybe this wasn't going to be the picnic I had anticipated. I was listening to the radio, and people were calling in saying that it seemed that gasoline was starting to run out and the prices were starting to run high.

I stopped at the nearest station and filled the thirsty gas tank that was good for about ten miles a gallon. When I first crossed the state line into Alabama, I could see evidence of the winds from Katrina that had come this far inland. Tall pine trees were bent to one direction, and the leaves on other trees seem to be pushed in the same direction and then seemingly hair-sprayed into place. They weren't moving much in the light breezes that now blew.

About fifty miles into Alabama, I saw the first line at a gas station. This was a BP station in the middle of a long stretch of interstate. Cars and RVs were lined up the exit ramp, down a short stretch of road, and into the station. I pulled over to get some video of the line, then walked over to the station where people were filling not just their cars, but those bright-red five- and ten-gallon gas cans.

One driver told me that people had started hearing that gas was going to become hard to find, so they were getting what they could while somebody still had it. I was happy with a couple of good interviews, but also started to feel like I was in for something for which I was not prepared. Did I bring any five- or ten-gallon gas tanks? No. Did a shortage of gas in a hurricane-ravaged area even occur to me? No.

By the time I had driven through Montgomery and Mobile and then crossed into Mississippi, I started to realize what I was facing. Even so, I kept going, knowing that I had a job to do, both professionally and personally.

On the personal front, my goal was to go to Waveland and find Bryan and Judy's house. They had fled Mississippi prior to the storm and were staying with my in-laws in South Carolina. They were very nervous about the fate of their home, particularly after some of the national broadcast and cable news organizations started getting pictures back from the Gulf. I had promised to shoot video of the house and get it on the news within a couple of days so that they could see if anything was left standing.

Professionally, my job was to find compelling stories and try to establish any Charlotte-area connections to the storm and its aftermath. With so much of the national media focused on New Orleans, I had decided not to go there, but instead to concentrate on the small towns near the Mississippi-Louisiana border.

When I got to the Waveland area it was late afternoon, but there were still several hours of sunlight. It was forty-eight hours after the storm had come through. I wish I had enough command of the English language to describe adequately the scenes that were before me, but I'll try here. Most people have seen images from Katrina, but nothing on television really did justice to the totality of the destruction.

If you stood outside on the street and looked around 360

degrees, you would not be able to find a scene that didn't include things that were broken, torn, or battered. You could not rest your eye on anything that looked normal.

On the interstate, there was an overturned conversion van. The windshield was shattered, and there was blood splattered around. It was just sitting beside the travel lane with no one around. Many of the big green exit and direction signs that line the interstates were either on the ground or twisted in what looked like impossible angles. Once you got off the interstate, the only trees left standing had had their leaves ripped free and most of their branches. The other trees were all over the ground and broken into kindling. Houses were flattened or flooded. Everywhere I saw steps that led to nowhere—three- and four-step brick, concrete, or wood steps that were meant to lead into the front door, but there was no front door to go in. Roofs of houses were blown off, lying broken on the ground. Shingles and bricks and random pieces of wood lay everywhere. I had to be careful walking because of all the wooden boards that had been peeled off people's houses had nails sticking up, and there was a lot of broken glass.

Cars and trucks had been flooded and still held pools of a nasty brown water that smelled as bad as anything I've ever breathed. All over the ground was a miry sort of clay, dark gray, almost green in color. It too had its own unforgettable stench and covered the roads. Since I was one of the first vehicles to drive in the area, I had to make tracks in it much like you do in a fresh snowfall.

Family pictures, hairbrushes, clothes, furniture, mini blinds, books, washers, and dryers—all evidence of human life—had been blown across the landscape and covered with the thin brown haze of the now dried-up water in which they had been immersed.

Then there were the people. In some neighborhoods, I didn't see a soul, but in others, people just walked around picking through the piles of rubbish. Very few paid attention to this big white TV truck driving slowly through the streets. In the town of Waveland, I came across a boat in the middle of a four-lane road. Everyone just drove around it. Like that wrecked van on the interstate, cleaning it up now just wasn't anyone's priority.

I passed the Waveland Police Department. Instead of police cars, I saw something like a Geo Tracker and maybe an old Chevy Lumina with handmade signs duct taped on the doors that said "Waveland PD." It was obvious that these officers were pressing their personal cars into service, making yet another sacrifice for the good of their fellow townspeople.

I thought I had remembered how to find Bryan and Judy's house. For the most part I was right, but I had to rely on my memory since street signs were knocked down and familiar landmarks no longer existed. I had to dodge flooded cars and downed power lines and trees to make my way down Waveland Avenue. When I turned onto that street, I feared the worst. Nearly every house that I saw was destroyed, and I feared the same for Bryan and Judy's small brown home. At first, I didn't think I'd be able to get down to their house. The road was blocked with limbs and branches, and that miry mess on the street was causing my tires to spin. I got out and moved some of the debris, then drove on.

The house, miraculously, was still standing. In fact, it was the only one on that block still standing. It had been moved several feet off the foundation, but it was still there, and from the outside, if you didn't know any better, it didn't appear to be damaged. The yard was a wreck, though. All the green grass was now a musty gray. All the bushes were gone, and debris from other homes was everywhere on the lawn. I ran around the side of the truck to get my camera and start shooting video, excited that I was going to be able to bring some good news to my worried family members. Then someone yelled at me.

"Hey, will you help us?" one of Bryan's neighbors called. He and another man were trying to get their old Lincoln Town Car out of the ditch on the side of the road. I asked how I could help, and they said they wanted me to drive down to the car in my van and tow it out. That would mean driving in the ever-deepening muck on the road, then trying to pull a large car out of a ditch. I didn't have any rope, and I was driving a brand-new live truck that cost the station well over $100,000. If that truck became stuck, then so would I, with no way out and nowhere to go. I told them I couldn't do it, that it wasn't my truck and that there was no way it wasn't going to get just as hung up as that Town Car. I still had a job to do, and a responsibility to my family and my employer.

The men weren't happy with my answer. I don't guess I blame them, but I still think it was the only choice I could make. The men cussed me pretty good, and one started walking toward me. The other men held him back, much to my relief. I let them continue to cuss me while I started shooting video of Bryan and Judy's house. I got a shot from the front, the side, and the back, then a wider shot of the yard. After that, I got back in the truck, slowly backed it up Waveland Avenue until I found some pavement not covered in muck, turned around, and drove away.

Bryan and Judy's house had been about a half mile from the

Gulf. Now, as far as I could tell, there were no more houses between it and the water. I drove back through Waveland, stopping every few blocks to shoot some video. I didn't have to be in a hurry to do that, as those scenes of distress and destruction weren't going anywhere.

I had less than half a tank of gas by now. I got back on the interstate and drove from Waveland to Gulfport. There I exited the interstate, thinking that surely in this town there was electricity and gasoline. I pulled into the parking lot of a Hampton Inn just off the highway. It was full of people, but I soon realized there was no power, no clean water, and, of course, no gas. I was down to less than a quarter of a tank now, and in one of those trucks, that will not take you very far. All the people were on the move, yet not really going anywhere, just walking around, looking here and there, going back to where they were a few minutes before. There was a tangible sense of hopelessness. The guests were people who fled the storm, thinking the damage wouldn't have reached this far. And now that small hotel room was the only home they had, and with no power or water or gas, they sat outside their rooms. Many had moved the cushioned chairs and loveseats from their room to the parking lot. The heat was stifling, the humidity nearly overwhelming, but with no power for the air conditioners, the parking lot at least offered the occasional gulf breeze.

It was right around six p.m. in Charlotte. I knew I was supposed to call in and do a live "phoner" for the six o'clock news. To my surprise, I did have cell phone service, so I made the call. The producer told the anchors I was there, so we went on the air. I described the destruction that I was witnessing, told them about the images I had seen and the people I had talked to. Then one of our anchors, Maureen

O'Boyle, noteworthy for having hosted the tabloid show *A Current Affair* in the 1990s, asked me how I was doing. I had to be honest. I told her that I was out of gas, out of food, and pretty hopeless—and that I really had no idea what I was going to do next. I know I sounded pitiful, but I also now think it was petulant. Compared to what the people around were facing, I had it pretty easy. I still had a place to go home to, still had a job, still had my life. Many of those around me couldn't make those claims.

My desperation must have been apparent to our viewers. Since that time, I've heard from more than one church in the Charlotte area that told me they prayed for me that night. My own church specifically prayed that I would somehow find gas.

I believe in the power of prayer, and I believe God answers our prayers in one of three ways: "Yes, no, and not now." I believe it is His divine wisdom that determines how those prayers will be answered in order to grow us as people. That's my sincere belief, but on that night, there was only one answer that I felt I could accept, and that would be to somehow, against the odds, find gas.

That quest didn't start well. I found a Gulfport police officer to ask his advice, and he told me he didn't know where there was gas within one hundred miles. Then he told me that I had better not stay there that night with the WBTV truck loaded with expensive electronic equipment. Since Katrina hit, he told me, the city had become "Dodge City." I learned later that several pawn shops had been broken into and that hundreds of guns had been stolen.

I only wish the irony of my plight had occurred to this officer. He was telling me not to stay here, yet there was no gas that would enable me to leave.

A while later, I spotted a highway patrolman. Realizing the chance I was taking by driving with a gas gauge moving closer and closer to *E*, I followed him about two miles to an intersection where he pulled over to speak with a local police officer. I apologized for the interruption and made my case, asking if there was any chance he knew where I could get enough gas to get back to Mobile, Alabama. Same answer as before: nowhere around here.

I drove back to the hotel parking lot, only this time I noticed a long line of cars at a gas station. That moment of hope soon faded: the station wasn't open, and the people were parking there in the hope that maybe by tomorrow they would be able to get gas. I sat in the truck and prayed. I talked to two volunteers with the Salvation Army who drove up. I even interviewed them. I turned down their offer of food, even though I was hungry. It just seemed to me that the food needed to go to the people who lived here, not somebody in the media who should have had enough sense to bring something to eat. I actually did have some snack food, a couple bottles of water, and some crackers that my wife was smart enough to pack for me, but I was still hungry.

The hunger in my stomach could not compete with that of my gas tank. That's really all I could think about. A local man walked up to the truck and started talking to me. I think he sensed that I was in a spot. He started telling me that there was this guy selling gas out of a tank he was carrying in his car. It was ten dollars a gallon, but he had a way of getting plenty of it. I told him I'd take all I could get into this beast and asked him what I needed to do. Now it hit me that I was encouraging and participating in black market gas, and enrich-ing someone who was obviously a dirtbag. At the moment, it didn't matter. I justified it by saying that when I got out of this mess, I'd do a story on the guy and expose this corruption and price gouging. Turns out the dirtbag was smarter than that. When he saw that I was in a television truck, he took off. So there was no gas for me, and no story either. Just as well.

I sat back in my driver's seat, back in my spot in the hotel parking lot, trying to figure out some way, any way, to get out of "Dodge City." Then I noticed something: Ford Crown Victorias were coming off the interstate and driving behind a grocery store across the street from where I was parked. There were troopers, deputies, unmarked cars, all driving behind that building, then after a few minutes, coming back out and hitting the road. I had to know what this was all about, so I cranked the engine and drove over to the store. As I eased behind the small, one-story cinderblock building, I saw that the cars in a line were getting gas from a handheld pump attached to a tank in the ground. It was the State of Mississippi's emergency fuel reserve. One of the men who was working the gas pump walked up and asked me what I wanted. I explained my situation and asked if there was any way he could spare a few gallons that I would happily pay for. He looked at the truck and said, "Well, this isn't exactly what you'd call an 'emergency vehicle.'"

I said, "Yeah, I know, but I don't know what else to do."

He looked around, then told me to pull up to one of the pumps after some of the police cars had driven off. When I got to the pump, he told me that he could provide me half a tank of gas. It turned out that I got three quarters of a tank, and for that I was beyond grateful. I tried to pay him, but he wouldn't accept it. He wished me well and told me to be careful. That's an act of kindness and an answered prayer that I will never forget.

That unexpected fill-up gave me enough gas to travel the seventy-five miles from Gulfport, Mississippi, to Mobile, Alabama. I drove around Mobile, shooting more video and doing a few interviews. Since a TV live truck is big, heavy, and not at all fuel efficient, it wasn't long before I needed another fill-up before trying to make my way back to Charlotte. Someone in Mobile told me that there was a gas station opened "across town" that did have gas and working pumps. I headed that way and joined a line of cars that stretched for miles into the parking lot of a gas station. The line moved so slowly that I kept the truck in park for long periods and climbed in the back to edit video. I had asked the driver of the car behind me to blow his horn each time the line moved, so that I could go back to the driver's seat and roll up a few more feet. During one of those moments that I was behind the wheel, I saw a car pull up to a stop sign at one of the intersections. A young woman was driving and I could see a small child in the car. We made eye contact, and she motioned to me that she was just trying to get across the intersection and not break into our gas pump line. I held up when the car in front of me moved ahead, but instead of pulling across the street, the woman pulled right into the line in front of me. I thought that was bad form, but didn't really think that much about it. What could I do?

Five minutes later, a man approached the driver's door of my truck, holding a handgun. In a profanity-laden tirade, he demanded to know why I had allowed that car to pull in front of me. He had been in one of the cars a few spots behind me and had seen me let the other driver in. I told him that I thought she was crossing the intersection and didn't know she was going to pull into our line until it was too late. He warned me against letting any other cars in the line and told me that if the gas pumps ran out before he was able to fill up, that he would hold me responsible. Then he waved the gun, offered a parting profane phrase, and returned to his car. Now I was praying again, this time that the gas station had enough fuel for me and for him. Fortunately, it did. I was able to fill up the tank and hit the road.

While in Mississippi, the station contacted me to let me know that there was a family in Concord, North Carolina, that had not heard from their elderly parents who lived along the Gulf Coast. They gave the station the address and asked if I could check on them. They were desperate for information. The address was about twenty miles from where I was, so I headed that way, praying the whole time. When I turned onto the street, the prospects were not good. Trees were down everywhere, the houses heavily damaged, and there were no people around. I drove the four blocks, avoiding limbs and muck that covered the road, until I reached the house. To my surprise and relief, it was still standing, and I found the couple working in the yard, trying to clean up the mess. They were very surprised to see a big TV truck roll up in the driveway. I told them who I was and why I was at their house, and they were thrilled. I interviewed them and shot video of them working. I managed to call the station later and got them to call the family in Concord and let them know that everyone was okay. The next night, they were able to see their parents on TV. That struck me as another one of those examples of me being in the very place God wanted me.

I went to Pascagoula, Mississippi, and spent several hours there. The town was devastated. I pulled into the parking lot of a large apartment complex where dozens of families stood outside. There was massive damage to the structure, no power, and no water. A broken water pipe shot a stream ten feet in the air, providing the only fun diversion for the many children who lived there. My truck was quickly surrounded by residents who said they needed help. They said they had not heard from any relief agencies or town officials and didn't know what to do. Even though my TV station was in Charlotte, they recognized that media coverage, any media coverage, could help them, and thankfully, it did. I called my hometown mayor, Susan Kluttz in Salisbury, and told her about Pascagoula. It didn't take long before Salisbury "adopted" Pascagoula and sent resources to the hurricane-ravaged community. The hospital in Salisbury helped the Pascagoula hospital, and schools in Rowan-Salisbury set up partnerships with schools in Pascagoula. Firefighters in Salisbury, police and sheriff's deputies from Rowan County, and many others went to that area to provide any help they could.

Six months later, I went back to do a follow-up story. I was amazed at the progress in some areas, and distressed at the lack of progress in others. Some communities looked the same as they appeared the day after Katrina struck. Huge trees were still down, wrecked vehicles were everywhere, and belongings such as family albums and clothes still littered the landscape.

My Katrina experience changed me in at least one way—I asked the station if I could get out of covering hurricanes. While there are some reporters who thrive on these types of exciting stories—the stinging rain in the face, the wind pushing you down the road, the desperate search for an open Waffle House—I just couldn't look at it like that any longer. The destruction and pain that I saw from

Katrina made it so that I only wanted to cover those storms if I could talk about what was being done to help people recover and how to better prepare for the wrath of the storm.

I was still assigned to cover a few more hurricanes after Katrina, but never experienced anything quite like that.

9: A Few Amazing People

Newlyweds Maryann and Marcus Kauffman

FOR OVER THIRTY-TWO YEARS, I'VE HAD THE privilege to meet and interview some people who have accomplished so much for both themselves and the world around them, sometimes under heartbreaking circumstances, and a few who have truly done the unexpected. I'd like to highlight a few in this chapter whose stories you might not know or remember.

Maryann and Marcus Kauffman

Newlyweds Marcus and Maryann Kauffman were returning to their home in western Rowan County in November 2013, when Marcus noticed something that looked out of place. There was a suspicious vehicle parked near their home that appeared to be broken-down. Marcus dropped Maryann off at a friend's house nearby, then returned to offer help to what he thought was a stranded driver. Instead, he discovered that people were stealing items from their home. He called 911 to report the incident, but during the conversation, told the dispatcher that shots were being fired. The call was then lost. Kauffman was found in his car with a gunshot wound to the back of his head, and the car crashed into a tree. Marcus Kauffman, a well-known volunteer firefighter, remained on life support for nearly three weeks after the shooting and died December 20 at Carolinas Medical Center in Charlotte.

One year after the shooting, Maryann agreed to do a formal interview with me. Her youthful appearance, long brown hair, and engaging smile that I had first seen in the weeks following the shooting were still there, even though her life had changed dramatically. In February, she gave birth to the couple's son, Landon. "He's just such a gift from God because I see God in him. I feel God's love through just giving me Landon," Maryann told me. "I love being a mom."

Maryann and Landon had moved back to Georgia, where she was born. Within that period of time, investigators were able to make arrests in the case. Jalend Daquan Turner, nineteen, and Khari Dewayne McClelland, twenty-three, were charged with first-degree murder; eighteen-year-old Tramel Devon Hart and twenty-five-year-old Michael Dwayne Teasley were charged with accessory after the fact to first-degree murder.

How did Maryann feel about the men who murdered her husband? "'For if you forgive men when they sin against you, your heavenly Father will also forgive you. But if you do not forgive men their sins, your Father will not forgive your sins,'" she quoted from the Bible, Matthew 6:14–15. "I don't see any exceptions in the Bible depending on how terrible the sin is, or how much it hurts me," she added. "Jesus forgave me; I can forgive them. Thank you all for caring, but please don't feel hate toward them on our behalf. I don't want that, and Marcus wouldn't want that."

The case against the suspects moved slowly over a period of years. Khari McClelland, who was facing the death penalty, pleaded guilty and was sentenced to life in prison in 2016. In 2017, Jaylend Turner pleaded guilty to second-degree murder, felony breaking and/or entering, felony larceny after breaking and/or entering, felony larceny of a firearm, and a recent charge of felony possession of a phone/communication device by inmate. Tramel Devon Hart was originally charged with accessory after the fact, but was sentenced to between six and seventeen months in prison after pleading guilty to a lesser charge. Hart did receive credit for the 1,038 days he spent in jail awaiting trial, according to Rowan County District Attorney Brandy Cook. Michael Dwayne Teasley pleaded guilty to possession of stolen goods and was sentenced to six to seventeen months in prison. Teasley was charged with being an accessory after the fact of murder.

Despite many in the community calling for the death penalty, particularly for McClelland, Maryann Kauffman insisted on grace and mercy. In a statement read in court, Kauffman said, "I just want to make it clear that I'm satisfied with this outcome. I'm definitely thankful we were able to avoid a trial. I want to thank everyone who has been involved these past few years with these cases. All of the time that was put into it, and not only that, but all of the genuine care and concern for us as a family. I would like for Jaylend Turner to know that I forgive him and that he's never too far from God's grace and love."

Each time I spoke with Maryann Kauffman, she exhibited the same grace and a profound inner peace. The life she had planned with her husband and child was senselessly shattered, yet she maintained a humble Christian character that left an impression on many who followed the case.

Dorris "Dee Dee" Wright

I came along a little too late to cover the major events of the Civil Rights Movement of the 1960s, but I was able to do stories with some of its major characters, including Reverend Jesse Jackson. One of these civil rights activists lives just a few blocks from me, and her name is Dee Dee Wright.

Dorris "Dee Dee" Wright was born in Greenville, South Carolina, and has been a civil rights activist since she was fifteen years old. In her book *The (W)right Thing*, she chronicles her participation in sit-ins at "whites only" lunch counters in Greenville. Wright was one of the Greenville Eight that challenged the segregation of the public library. In the landmark Supreme Court case Edwards v. South Carolina, Wright was one of the defendants. The case concluded with the court ruling that the students had exercised their constitutional rights in their protest of segregation.

It all began when Wright was a high school student in 1957. One day, like Rosa Parks, she boarded a city bus for the ride home. In her book, Wright wrote that she didn't know there was a colored section on the bus, so she sat down at an aisle seat, and a white girl sitting next to her pushed her stack of textbooks to the floor. Wright slapped her. The girl told the bus driver what happened. He drove to the police station and returned with an officer who removed Wright and the white girl from the bus.

"Yet during the time the white student and I spent in the police station lobby waiting to be freed, we learned something about ourselves and each other. It helped bridge society's divide," Wright wrote.

From that encounter, Wright would go on to have a distinguished life as a champion for civil rights. After living in several states, Wright settled in my hometown of Salisbury. As a reporter, I came into contact with her several times. She served as the head of the city planning commission and was instrumental in local groups that worked with police and other agencies to address racial disparities.

Wright came to Salisbury in 1988 to care for Elizabeth Duncan Koontz. The two had developed a friendship over the years. Koontz was another remarkable and inspiring woman, having served as Assistant State Superintendent of Schools in North Carolina and appointed by then President Richard Nixon to head the United States Department of Labor Women's Bureau. A school in Rowan County was named in her honor. After Koontz died in 1989, Wright began serving in various ways on local boards and commissions.

With her long and straight hair, Wright appeared younger than her years when I first met her. She is kind and gracious, but also a person who sets her mind on tasks and is a force to be reckoned with when she's passionately advocating for those who may not have a voice.

Dixonville was an African-American community in Salisbury that thrived in the mid-twentieth century. There were homes, churches, a school, businesses, and a cemetery. While most everything else went away over the years, the cemetery remained. Significantly, it was the first city-owned cemetery for the burial of African-Americans. While doing research for several stories related to the cemetery, I learned that local historian Betty Dan Spencer discovered that there were 500 documented burials at the cemetery. The oldest gravesite known is that of Mary Valentine, who died in 1851.

"This supports the supposition that African-Americans may have been interred on the property before the city of Salisbury purchased the acres for a cemetery on September 30, 1874," Spencer wrote. Other prominent African-American Salisburians are buried there, including Bishop John Jamison Moore, who founded the AME Zion Church in western North Carolina, and the Reverend Harry Cowan, a minister who was born into slavery, but went on to establish forty-nine churches and baptize 8,500 people.

Wright and several other local leaders began a project prior to 2010 to refurbish the cemetery, document the burials, and provide historical markers and signs to encourage visitors. In 2010, after requests from citizens, former Salisbury Mayor Susan Kluttz initiated the Dixonville-Lincoln Memorial Task Force to create the community memorial.

The task force worked for years on design plans and researching history, as well as raising money for the project. Wright put together a special event called Ministers of Comedy, a one-night event where a big crowd gathered to hear local ministers attempt to do stand-up comedy. It was a lot of fun, and the ministers were very funny, whether they intended to be or not.

One unfortunate incident marred the effort to recreate this local memorial. In February 2022, more than a dozen graves in the Dixonville Cemetery were vandalized, with tombstones knocked over and broken into pieces. I stood in the cemetery that afternoon and spoke with Wright about what had happened and the disappointment she felt. "At first I was stunned, then I thought about when are we going to be able to rest in peace?" Wright told me. "I think it's very important that we continue to honor those who have died and who are hopefully resting, in spite of what happened today, or whenever it happened," added Wright. "Yes, we will fix this. I mean, we are strong and we were at the closing where we were getting ready to have the final rededication of this cemetery, and somebody thought maybe this shouldn't be. But it will be—we will continue and we will fight for what we believe is right and is righteous."

Despite that temporary setback, much work was done by many to bring about the formal dedication of the cemetery in September 2023. I was honored to have been chosen to emcee this special event.

In summing up her life of service, Wright wrote in her book, "My goals in life have always been to help others, build bridges, and be a part of effective change." To this day, she continues to work toward this goal.

Haylee Gardner Shuping

Haylee Gardner Shuping did not seek a place in the spotlight. She came to prominence in the most unwelcome way possible.

Haylee was married to Jason Shuping. Jason was an officer with the Concord Police Department, and during his eighteen months of service, he received several commendations for going above and beyond his duties.

On December 16, 2020, twenty-five-year-old Shuping responded to a call involving a possible vehicle theft near a fast-food restaurant just off I-85. While confronting and exchanging gunfire with the suspect, Shuping was shot and killed. His partner was wounded. The suspect was shot and killed.

Once again, I was covering a difficult story. In situations like this, reporters need to be sensitive to the families of those involved, sensitive to the members of the local law enforcement agencies that just lost one of their own, but also dedicated to finding out the facts of the case. That can be a difficult line to walk. I did several stories following Shuping's death. Some were following up with new information about the incident, others highlighted the community's support for the officers and families. I reported on the Cabarrus Chamber of Commerce giving out thousands of blue light bulbs for residents to put in porch lights, on Shuping being honored by the President of the United States, and on the petition that eventually led to a bridge being named in Shuping's honor. His call number, 4434, was officially retired by the City of Concord as a reminder of his dedication to serving his community.

Over the years, I saw Haylee Shuping at several events honoring her late husband. She attended many such events, but to me, always looked uncomfortable and wary of the media. I couldn't blame her for feeling that way. She had been thrust into a heartbreaking situation, and therefore I didn't approach her because I understood that she was not comfortable speaking with the media. In May 2021, on the day Jason Shuping was honored posthumously with the Concord Police Medal of Valor and Purple Heart awards, I reached out to Lynn Shuping, Jason's mother. She replied, saying, "Our family truly appreciated the support from the community and the many ways the Concord Police Department and local officials have honored Jason and his dedication as an officer. Obviously, we would forego any honors or awards just to have Jason back with us. As his mother, I beg our community to stop the killing!"

I later learned that during this time, Haylee Shuping was working to create something that wouldn't just honor the life of her husband, but that would benefit the community in extraordinary ways. What she was doing was very important, and I really wanted to tell her story. After reading an interview she gave to *The Charlotte Observer*, I felt as if she had found her footing and perhaps a comfort level with speaking to reporters. In November 2022, I finally reached out to Haylee and asked for an interview. I promised to be as sensitive as possible, but explained that I thought her efforts should be recognized. To my surprise, she agreed to sit down and speak with me.

I was able to get permission from a local coffee shop to set up for the interview. I arrived early, picked out a good spot, then set up the camera and lights so that when Haylee walked in, she could just sit down, clip on the microphone, and have a conversation. Being so near the anniversary of Jason's death, I knew she may be thinking about that, and I just wanted to make things as comfortable as possible for her.

When she came in, she was gracious and friendly, with a beautiful smile. The hesitation I had seen in the past appeared to have been replaced with confidence. "Today is December the first, so today, you know, is a very hard day. It's going to be a very hard month, but I really just try to focus on finding support with my friends and family and the community and continuing on and honoring his legacy as well," Haylee told me.

We talked about the things she had been doing over the previous two years to honor the memory of her husband and to create positive change. To keep her husband's legacy alive, Haylee established a $25,000 scholarship at Rowan-Cabarrus Community College. She told me that she and Jason had actually talked about what they could do to help deserving students who wanted to become law enforcement officers. She said she knew Jason would be happy about what came from those conversations.

"I established the Officer Jason Shuping Public Safety Scholarship at Rowan-Cabarrus Community College to award deserving Basic Law Enforcement Training students financial access to the program." Shuping said in our interview on WBTV that she wanted to support those who wouldn't otherwise be able to take part in the program, and therefore add new law enforcement talent to Rowan and Cabarrus counties. Since her husband's death, Haylee Shuping has spent time with families of lost police officers, organized and attended events in Jason's memory, and started her own company. Shuping has done all of those things while earning an MBA from Wake Forest University. These efforts, Haylee told me, had helped her to grow and find new ways to do what's most important to her while serving her community and honoring the memory of her husband.

Jimmy Murphey

Any rookie news reporter knows that at the beginning of your career, you're going to get the worst schedule possible. The news never stops, of course, and that includes overnights and holidays. When I first became a full-time reporter with WBTV, I knew that it would mean working at times when everyone else would be off. It comes with the job that you will miss family moments and milestones until you've put in your years, and the natural attrition pushes you up the ladder. I worked several Christmas Days, Thanksgiving Days, and New Years, until I had the seniority to be able to get those days off. Well, most of the time. Working the holidays and being away from my family wasn't fun, but there were times that it paid off in unexpected ways.

When I first met Jimmy Murphey of Concord, it was right before Christmas of 1994. I had done my first on-air story as a reporter in April, so as a "newbie," I was going to have to work on that Christmas Day, and my assignment was to cover the annual meal that Murphey and a crew of volunteers prepared and gave away to the community. It was a tradition that began in 1932 with Jimmy's mother as a way to give to those around her and her family during the Depression. Jimmy carried it on until his health began to fail in 2008, when he was eighty. The annual Christmas dinner carried on for two years after his death until it was stopped in 2020.

I was not familiar with this tradition when I was assigned to cover it in 1994. I arranged to interview Jimmy a few weeks before Christmas to learn about how he was able to get enough food for the thousands of people that would be fed onsite at a local church hall, pick up a carry-out box, or have their meal delivered. Murphey lived in a small, old house on Woodsdale Street in Concord, a narrow street with lots of older houses. I arrived and met Jimmy, a tall African-American man with a loud voice, a firm handshake, and an ever-present cigarette. He invited me in and showed me stacks and stacks of canned food that he had already been collecting for the annual meal. He was getting donations from individuals and from companies, large and small. With enthusiasm, he shared the history of the annual Christmas dinner, but told me he was worried that his donations were down this year for the food and the toys. Toys? I wasn't aware of that part of it, but Jimmy told me that on every Christmas Eve, he gave away toys in his front yard. He collected hundreds of toys, new and used, and stored them in the small house. On Christmas Eve, he put the toys on rows of tables in the yard, then allowed families and individuals to walk along the rows and select one or two toys per person.

This first visit served as the template for stories I would do over the next several years. It always began a few weeks before Christmas, when Jimmy would tell me that donations were down and that he was worried that there wouldn't be enough to go around. After the story aired on TV, people would come through and fill up his small house and any other place he could find for storage. Jimmy counted on me to be a partner in his efforts, and that was fine by me. If I hadn't called him by Thanksgiving each year, he would call me, asking, "Where are you?"

For years, I covered the toy giveaway, and then the Christmas meal the next day. A typical story on the toy giveaway would include video showing cars and people lined up on narrow Woodsdale Street with police directing traffic. It greatly inconvenienced the other residents on Woodsdale who had a hard time getting in and out of their driveways, but since it was only one day a year, they mostly put up with it and planned accordingly.

"At the present time, it is about 2,000 people lining up now all the way from downtown to Woodsdale," Jimmy said on Christmas Eve, 2008. There were so many people in line that day that Jimmy had to enforce some ground rules to keep people from cutting in line or trying to go back through a second time. As it turned out, that was the last toy giveaway, due to Jimmy's failing health.

"I am going out glorious. I want to thank the people of Cabarrus County. Thank you and may God bless you and merry Christmas," said a tearful Murphey.

The first time I ever covered the annual Christmas dinner was an experience. There were rows and rows of tables set up. Dozens of volunteers ran around the large dining hall taking care of guests, working in the back to prepare food, or picking up food for deliveries all over Cabarrus County. Jimmy was the ringmaster over all he surveyed in that setting. With a tendency to micromanage, Jimmy would sometimes scold volunteers for not giving enough food or giving too much. He was constantly in motion from the dining room to the kitchen and back again. The volunteers took it all in stride, knowing that Jimmy's bark was much worse than his bite, and knowing that they were working toward the same goal.

"Anything I can do to help and ease their burden, I am there," Murphey told me.

Jimmy's contributions to the community were appreciated. In 2010, donations were collected to show that appreciation in a most tangible way: by building Murphey a brand-new house. The project included the demolition of Murphey's 1960s house—with floors that sagged due to the weight of all those donations over the years—and the construction of the new one on the same property. Murphey had already moved out of the old house and in with a neighbor when he could no longer keep up with all the repairs that were needed. In November 2010, I got to see Jimmy Murphey move into his new house, just in time for the holidays.

Murphey enjoyed nearly eight years in his new house, spending hours in the rocking chair on the front porch. He passed away in April 2018 at the age of eighty-eight.

The lesson in the story for me was another example of how local media can make a difference. Jimmy relied on me to tell his story every year, and as soon as we reported it, the donations would start pouring in. By following up and showing the events on Christmas Eve and Christmas Day, it gave a nice bit of attention not only to Jimmy, but to the dozens of volunteers who were sacrificing time with their families on a holiday in order to help out a genuinely wonderful cause.

10: Jimmie and Mary

My friend and former coworker Mike Rode as we worked the pits during a race week at Charlotte Motor Speedway.

COVERING CHARLOTTE MOTOR SPEEDWAY WAS AS MUCH about news as sports. There are estimates that each Cup race weekend at the track generates more than $100 million in economic impact. Thousands of jobs have been created and are sustained by racing. The Cabarrus County Convention Visitors Bureau said in 2019 that motorsports generated more than $450 million in economic impact across the region. It's a big part of the culture of the area too.

For years, the speedway left a gate open near the main entrance. It was used for fans who just wanted to stop by and walk out to the grandstands to get a look at the track. During the week and most every day, you could find fans who came by the track and just walked up the ramp and sat in the stands. Often, they could watch drivers from racing schools, such as the Richard Petty Driving Experience, have fun out on the track. But even on days when no one is on the track, the fans would still come.

Some days during racing's offseason or during a break, the NASCAR teams come to the track to run tire tests for Goodyear. Hundreds of fans typically show up on these days. There's no charge to sit in the stands, and they are sometimes treated to seeing their favorite drivers run lap after lap.

That's what brings me to this story and one of the most rewarding experiences I've ever had as a reporter.

The producers at WBTV sent photographer Mike Rode and me to the track to look for a story one Goodyear-tire-test day. Like me, Rode is a big fan of NASCAR racing and knows the sport well. As we began the assignment, I didn't really know what the angle of our story would be. Often the producers would trust me to just go out and find something. I appreciated that level of trust—or laziness! Either way, it was okay by me.

When we got to CMS, there was a fine mist in the air and no cars on the track. NASCAR Cup cars can't run in the rain for these tire tests, so all the cars and drivers were holed up in the garage area waiting for a break in the weather. Mike and I went into the stands where there were several hundred fans. In our business, doing interviews with regular people is sometimes called an "MOS," or "Man on the Street." That's where you just find a random person to ask an opinion about a particular subject. Sometimes those make for great stories, other times they're horrible. You may find someone who is articulate and passionate about the topic, or someone who can only manage one-word answers or responses that stray away from the topic of the story. On this day, there would be no disappointment. Mike started shooting video of fans in the stands. I hadn't really picked out anyone to interview yet, I was just letting him get the video we needed for the story. That's when Mike pointed out this one particular woman, likely in her sixties, sitting in the stands bundled up in a Jimmie Johnson fleece blanket. She was all-in on the Jimmie Johnson fan gear, as she also had a Jimmie Johnson hat, and, if I'm not mistaken, a Jimmie Johnson jacket. Johnson was at the track that day for the tire test, and she was there to cheer him on. I knew then I had the genesis for a story, but it would turn into much more.

Mike got a few shots of the woman watching the cars sitting on pit road waiting for the track to dry. The shots were good because she didn't realize that we were there, or that we were pointing the camera at her. Usually if someone realizes they may be on camera, they will change their expression: they may laugh, make a face, stiffen up, or turn their head away. In this case, her expression was totally natural. Once that was finished, we walked over to see if we could do a quick interview. When we got to the section of the grandstand where she was sitting, we were surprised to find that she was in a wheelchair. We introduced ourselves and I asked her if we could talk to her on camera. Graciously, she said that would be fine.

I asked her name. She replied that she was Mary Helms from Mount Airy, North Carolina. I asked my usual inane and obvious questions. "Who are you here to see?" "Are you a big fan?" I don't know exactly how it came about, but at some point, she mentioned that she was dying. She told me that cancer would likely take her life within the next year, so she was doing some things she really enjoyed while she was still able. Her son had brought her to the track so she could see her favorite driver.

The wheels on the cars still weren't turning, but the wheels in my head were. That misty rain also meant the drivers probably weren't doing anything right now. "Mary, have you ever met Jimmie?" I asked.

"No, but I would love to," she said.

My eyes locked with Mike's. We were both thinking the same impossible thought. I turned and walked off, leaving Mike to shoot some more video of Mary. The rain had now started to fall a little heavier.

Adrian Parker worked for the public relations department at CMS at the time. He's a great guy and always helpful. I knew that what I was asking was going to be a real stretch, but I called him and told him about Mary. I asked, "Is there any way we can get Jimmie Johnson and Mary together for just a minute?"

There was a pause on the line as Adrian considered. Then he said, "Give me two minutes and I'll call you back." I hung up, thinking now that somehow this just might happen. Thirty seconds later, the phone rang back. "Can you get her to the media center in ten minutes?" Adrian asked.

I would make it happen.

The media center is in the infield of the track. We were at the top of the grandstand near the start-finish line. To get to the media center from the grandstand takes a while. You can't simply go across the track; you have to go around it, through a tunnel that runs beneath the backstretch, then along a road in the infield that leads to the media center. I ran back to Mike and Mary, and her son had joined us by now. I let him in on what we were going to do, and he was good with it. I then turned to Mary. I didn't tell her what would be waiting for her, but I asked her if she could take a little ride with me. She looked puzzled, but agreed to go. With the help of her son, we moved Mary and her wheelchair out of the stands and down to my car. Her son took the wheelchair while Mary rode with me. Her son followed, with Mike in a big WBTV live truck right behind.

As I pulled up to the parking spaces at the media center, there was Jimmie Johnson, standing with Adrian. Mary didn't recognize him at first; it seemed to be the last thing she was expecting. As I opened the passenger door to my car, I told Mary that I had someone I wanted her to meet. Then it hit her. There stood Jimmie Johnson— she was thrilled! She began laughing merrily as I helped her out of the car and back into the wheelchair.

The seven-time NASCAR Cup Racing Champion, still wearing his driving suit, walked over to Mary. They hugged and talked for a few minutes. Johnson was very kind and genuinely seemed to enjoy this fan moment. Mike and I stood back a few feet to shoot the video we needed, not wanting to be too intrusive. After they talked, Mary asked Jimmie if he could sign an autograph or two, and he happily obliged. I think he signed every article of clothing Mary had and didn't mind a bit.

On the ride back out of the infield, Mary was just over the top with excitement. When she had left Mount Airy with her son that morning, she said the best she hoped for was to be able to see Jimmie run a few laps. She ended up with much more. It was the kind of interaction most fans can only dream about.

Mary died from cancer a few years later. I received a note from her son shortly after, telling me how that moment at Charlotte Motor Speedway had been something she always wanted to talk about. He even told me that the pastor mentioned the encounter during her memorial service.

A few months after that, I had the chance to interview Jimmie again. After the interview, I asked if he remembered meeting the lady at the media center. He flashed a quick smile and said he certainly did remember it and that it was one of his favorite moments with a fan. I told him that she had passed away, but that his kindness on that day was something that she never forgot.

You realize as a reporter that there are certain things that you can make happen that can make a difference in the world. The main thing I did that day was to just take the available elements—Mary, Jimmie Johnson, Adrian Parker—and find a way to connect them. Once that happened, it produced something truly special for us all.

11: Erica Parsons II

This photo of Erica Parsons, given to me by her biological mother Carolyn, is one of the few with Erica smiling.

WHEN THE NEWS FIRST BROKE THAT ERICA Parsons was missing, she had been missing for more than a year and a half, and people had lots of questions. Who was she? How did she seem to live off the grid when her other family members were going about their lives? The story that adoptive parents Sandy and Casey Parsons had told about Erica going to live with her grandmother Nan was immediately questioned by law enforcement. They could find no record of "Nan," and Sandy and Casey Parsons told investigators and reporters that they delivered Erica to a fast-food restaurant in Mooresville, North Carolina, where she was picked up by Erica's biological grandmother Irene "Nan" Goodman. They claimed Erica later called and said that she did not want to return to Salisbury. A few weeks after telling this story, Casey Parsons admitted that she may have been duped by the woman she said was posing as "Nan."

Within months, the case attracted national media attention. The

FBI and the National Center for Missing and Exploited Children became involved. Casey and Sandy Parsons went on national television on *Dr. Phil*, and Sandy failed a lie detector test when asked if he knew what happened to Erica.

And for those of us covering the story locally, it turned out there were some people who remembered Erica. After getting a tip from a former staff member at a public school in September 2013, I was able to confirm through school records that Erica Parsons attended Bostian Elementary School in Rowan County from August 2003 until July 2004. The paperwork indicated that she left Bostian for Shadybrook Elementary in Kannapolis in 2004.

"I remember that I saw her individually sometime [sic]. I remember her smile and how she brushed her bangs out of her eyes if she felt anxious," the staffer said. "She would beam when praised, and she was hesitant when she thought she might not know the answer to a question—that's when she would brush her bangs away from her eyes and puff air out of her mouth. I recall how she tilted her head to one side and would smile and that she loved stickers. I guess I wanted to add those things that I remember, because I find it terribly sad that no one that knew Erica has named her favorite color or game or music group or TV show or place to go out to eat."

Now, instead of just a small face with brown eyes and short, dark hair that stared blankly back from a handful of photographs given to us by the family, Erica Parsons had a life.

I and other reporters worked to mine every detail we could find about Erica, her family, and what investigators were discovering.

Erica Parsons was adopted when she was two years old by Sandy and Casey Parsons in 2000. She was given to them by her biological mother, Carolyn, who believed Sandy and Casey would be better able to create a stable home for Erica. Carolyn had once been married to Sandy's brother William Steve Parsons, II. To this day, Carolyn feels guilt for unknowingly handing her little girl over to her executioners.

There were several searches conducted by law enforcement, both at the Miller Chapel Road home where Erica lived with Casey and Sandy and their other children, as well as at a property owned by Sandy's father, William Parsons. A home in Rockwell, North Carolina, where the family lived prior to moving to Miller Chapel Road was also searched. If anything was found, investigators did not say.

"Quit lying to everybody and come forward with what you've done to my child. Or find my child and bring her to me," Carolyn Parsons told Sandy and Casey Parsons when I interviewed her in November 2013. "I wish I knew more. I wish I knew where she was. I wish I knew how to go get her, and hold her, and hug her, and kiss her, and give her all the love that she never had."

Carolyn Parsons made a personal appeal to her daughter during our interview, saying, "If you are still out there—whether it be me, or whether it be somebody else—even if you're happy where you are, just please let somebody know that you're alive and that you're okay."

She had more words for Sandy and Casey, adding, "You know what you did to my daughter, whether it be good or whether it be bad. You need to open your mouth and you need to come forward. And you need to tell somebody."

In late 2013, I was able to obtain a series of emails between Carolyn Parsons and Casey Parsons. Carolyn later confirmed that the emails were legitimate. They covered nearly two years of communication, from April 2010 through March 2012, with Carolyn frequently asking about how Erica was doing and requesting to see her. Casey shared stories with Carolyn about Erica in school, taking driver's ed, and growing up. Casey always had an excuse for not letting Carolyn see Erica.

We now know that Erica Parsons was dead by January 2012, but at the time, Carolyn thought she was still alive. She wrote an email to Casey saying, "*could u please send me a recent picture of erica its been sense 2010…id love a ic r t see her agin if she would also tell her happy early 15 bday please thanks.*"

Casey replied several hours later, saying, "*Carolyn, Erica is doing perfect. Don't know why all these rumors are floating around about where she is. Sandy & I still have full custody of Erica and she is our daughter. Erica is still OUR daughter. I haven't sent pictures of any updates because Erica has asked me not to.*"

Several days later, Casey emailed Carolyn again, this time saying, "*I talked with Erica all last night. She is making progress.*" She later adds, "*You are like a sister to me. You trusted me with Erica and I hope you still do. I would give my life for this young lady. She is turning into a very beautiful young lady.*"

The emails continued through March 2012, with Casey telling Carolyn that Erica had gotten her learner's permit and that they had to buy special "pedal extensions for her." Carolyn replied that she hoped she would be able to see Erica in April. How could she know that Erica had been dead and buried in a shallow grave for months?

After her adoptive brother reported Erica missing, the community was organizing prayer vigils and putting up posters on light poles all over the county with Erica's picture. The FBI created an age-enhanced picture to show what Erica might look like at the age of fifteen, since all the available pictures showed her as much younger. That image was used on posters, given to reporters, and placed on at least one large billboard.

In August 2013, a team of investigators with the Rowan Sheriff's Office, the North Carolina State Bureau of Investigation, the FBI, and District Attorney Brandy Cook met and made the decision to focus on the money that Casey and Sandy Parsons had been receiving in federal adoption funds for a girl who had been missing for more than a year. That was a productive angle in the investigation that eventually led to the conclusion of the case.

Shortly after that meeting, I received a tip about what was discussed. After verifying it, I wrote an article for the WBTV website explaining the potential financial crimes that had taken place, and that it could lead to charges for Casey and Sandy. Sandy and Casey were much more likely to face fraud charges than anything to do with harming Erica since there was no physical evidence, I concluded. Within hours of the story being posted, I received a hateful email from Casey threatening a lawsuit over the allegations. My relationship with Casey and Sandy had been awkward, but now was broken. I still had to be able to speak with them as the days, months, and years went on, but I also knew that they were very likely guilty of horrible crimes against a child. That was one of those times where, as a reporter, I had to maintain objectivity, but as a person, I had a strong conviction that they were murderers.

I dug into their backgrounds. Sandy Wade Parsons was born in December 1973. He was less than six feet tall, overweight, with short reddish-brown hair and a neatly trimmed beard. Casey Stone Parsons was born in January 1975. She was about the same height as

Sandy and also overweight. Her hair was shoulder-length or longer, light brown, sometimes straight, but usually curly. The couple had five children of their own: son Wade, born in 1992; son Jamie, born in 1992; daughter Brooklyn, born in 1995; daughter Sadie, born in 2004; and son Toby, born in 2006. Erica, born on February 24, 1998, joined the family in July 2000.

According to court testimony, Sandy worked several jobs, including as a department manager in a grocery store.

I spent many hours parked across the street from the Parsons home in Rowan County, or in the driveway of a friendly neighbor. I set up my camera and just observed as Sandy, Casey, and the other adult family members came and went. On some days, they would come out and scream or make obscene gestures at me, and on other days, they kept the doors closed and curtains drawn. It seemed to be a useless vigil on my part, but I had to stay with it. My news director shifted other reporters around to cover stories in my area while I stayed camped at that house. The story was so high profile, and the family so unpredictable, that we didn't want to take the chance of missing anything. It may have seemed like overkill until the day I saw the large U-Haul truck in the driveway. Casey and Sandy were moving their belongings out of the house and into that truck and several other vehicles. I found out they were moving from Rowan County to Fayetteville in order to escape the media attention.

On that day, I was standing with my camera in the yard directly across the street from the Parsons driveway. There was a newspaper reporter and photographer standing with me and another TV crew a few feet down. After loading up a few items, Sandy Parsons got behind the wheel of the U-Haul. He started the engine, pulled out of the driveway, then drove directly across the street toward us. The other media members scrambled, but for some reason, I was frozen and didn't move. I had my eye on the viewfinder of the camera. The truck came into the yard and stopped inches from my camera. It was so close, that the only image in the viewfinder was of the GMC logo on the front of the grill. I didn't say a word. After a few tense seconds, Sandy backed up and drove away. The next day, I was right back in the same spot to watch them move more items. Sandy came at me again, only this time he was walking, smiling, and apologizing. I had my camera up on the tripod, so I reached back and started recording.

"I apologize," he said. "I was just frustrated with the helicopters, and I was getting phone calls when I was doing all that yesterday—from the cops saying people were calling them, ringing the phone off the hook, saying we were running.

"The only thing I want right now is Erica to call home, tell us she's safe, and get my two babies," he said. "Nobody realizes that there's two small kids involved in this that do want to come home."

The two younger biological children of Sandy and Casey had been taken by the Department of Social Services a few days earlier.

"No judge in Rowan County will give me my kids back while this is going on," Parsons said. "And people riding by shouting death threats, stuff like that, it just brings out the weirdos. They're flipping me off, hollering. I'm getting weird phone calls. You ought to hear some of the phone calls I got," he said. "One at one thirty in the morning, some woman, creepy voice, telling me she wants to kill me."

Sandy Parsons said at that time that he was convinced that Erica Parsons was still alive, but afraid to call and let anyone know where she was or how she was doing. "There's been sightings, I've had family members call me recently and say there was a sighting at a rest stop," he claimed. "We asked, 'Why didn't you call the cops? Don't wait and call us—call the cops!'"

He wanted me to know how much he loved and missed Erica. He rolled up his sleeve to show me a tattoo on his bicep. It was a ribbon with initials of his children, including an ELP for Erica Lynn Parsons.

Parsons also hinted that "the whole story" about Erica's disappearance would eventually come out. That turned out to be the one thing he said that was truthful.

On July 30, 2014, my rock-solid prediction from that tip I received came to fruition. The FBI paid an early morning visit to the new Fayetteville home of Sandy and Casey Parsons and arrested them on seventy-six counts of fraud charges.

Jamie Parsons, Erica's adoptive brother who set the investigation in motion exactly one year earlier when he reported Erica missing, told one of our reporters that federal agents kicked the door in, guns drawn, when they came to serve the warrants on his parents. He also said that over the previous two days, his mother indicated that she knew she was going to be arrested.

"Momma said she knew that they were coming. She had a feeling they were coming," Jamie said.

That afternoon, I was able to get hold of the federal indictments. They said that from February 2010 to August 2013, Sandy and Casey committed tax fraud, mail fraud, theft of government funds, identity theft, and engaged in a conspiracy to defraud the government. The couple received government-funded adoption assistance, Medicaid,

Social Security payments, and Food and Nutrition Services benefits for a dependent that did not live with them, and used the mail to commit the fraud.

I was in Salisbury when I heard this, so I immediately rushed to be outside the federal courthouse in Winston-Salem forty-five minutes away, because I knew that's where they would be brought to appear for arraignment. I was only there for a few minutes when I saw a white van coming up the street and turning into the entrance to the courthouse. Sandy and Casey were inside that van. They appeared before a federal judge at 2:30 p.m. that afternoon, asking for, and receiving, court-appointed attorneys.

The government requested each be held in prison on a $25,000 secured bond, meaning they'd be able to get out of prison by posting $2,500. They told the judge they would not be able to get that amount of money. They did get out, however, when the judge changed the bond arrangements.

More and more information was coming out about the bizarre behavior of Casey Parsons, even before Erica was in her care. Amy Miller, a Michigan woman, said she hired Casey Parsons to be her surrogate and carry her child in August 2001. Miller says Parsons claimed to have had a miscarriage, but didn't. Five months later, Miller was finally able to track down Parsons and take home her son. She had the DNA test to prove that the child was hers.

Documents and statements indicated the investigators firmly believed that Erica Parsons was dead. But it would take another two years and the prison separation of Sandy from Casey to finally answer that question.

12: Sports Celebrities

Richard and Kyle Petty surprised me with a retirement party at Charlotte Motor Speedway just a few weeks before I did my last story. They looked a lot better in the cowboy hats than I did, but it was one of the most unforgettable moments of my career.

DOING STORIES WITH SPORTS PERSONALITIES WAS a highlight of my career. The worlds of news and sports frequently intersect and that gave me the chance to meet some big names. Cal Ripken Jr., Hall of Fame NFL linebacker Willie Lanier, wrestling legend Ric "Nature Boy" Flair, Tiger Woods, and NHRA drag racing icon John Force are among those I've been able to spend a few minutes with in an interview setting. And since Charlotte is NASCAR country, I've met and interviewed nearly every current NASCAR driver and quite a few of the legends.

NASCAR Hall of Famer Bobby Allison holds a special place in my heart. I interviewed him at Charlotte Motor Speedway a few years ago. He suffers from memory loss due to a serious accident he had at the Pocono Raceway a number of years ago that ended his career as a driver. As we were talking, I asked him about some memories of races he ran at Charlotte Motor Speedway, including a win in the October race in 1985. He struggled to remember, and then just told me that he simply had no recollection of that race. I felt awful, so much so that it choked me up. I apologized profusely. Bobby told me to stop; he said it was fine, that this kind of thing happened all the time and that it didn't bother him. He was so gracious about the whole thing, and I was struck by it.

One day, out of the blue, I was standing outside my bureau in Salisbury when Bobby, his wife Judy, and another couple walked over from the ice cream shop across the street. I kept looking at him, thinking, *That's crazy. Why would Bobby Allison, the legendary leader of The Alabama Gang, be walking around in downtown Salisbury?* His wife Judy noticed me staring. She smiled and said, "Yeah David, it's him." That really got me flummoxed; first of all it confirmed that it was Bobby Allison, but how did his wife know my name? They came over and talked for a few minutes, and it turned out that they actually lived in the area and watched our news programs. Being recognized by Judy and Bobby Allison I count as a badge of honor to this day.

My devotion to my job doesn't trump my devotion to my family, and often that means there are events that I miss so that I can be at home. I don't regret those decisions for a minute, but if I had chosen to go to Charlotte Motor Speedway instead of home, I would have had the chance to see and interview Jessica Alba, Pamela Anderson, Anna Kournikova, and yes, believe it or not, Carmen Electra.

I did see SpongeBob SquarePants. He was walking into the media center at CMS with two assistants. I think maybe he can't see too well, or maybe it was just being out of Bikini Bottom for so long, but the assistants were guiding him through the door while he held his arms out to the side. It probably didn't take him long to realize that the media center didn't serve Krabby Patties.

Guenther Steiner was, until January 2024, the team principal for the Haas Formula One Team. The team principal runs the team, manages day-to-day operations, and generally carries as much of the responsibility for the team's success as its drivers. It's the only US-based F1 team, and the headquarters are in Kannapolis on the same large campus as Stewart-Haas Racing's NASCAR team. I've been a NASCAR fan for as long as I can remember and knew next to nothing about F1.

If you don't know much about Formula One either, F1 is the richest motorsports circuit in the world. Grand Prix races are run in more than a dozen countries and attract millions of fans to see these drivers battle wheel-to-wheel on demanding road courses. I got a quick education in F1 in 2014 when industrialist Gene Haas announced the formation of the Haas F1 team. He made his money as the founder of Haas Automation, a machine tool manufacturer. I covered the press conferences and threw myself into learning about the sport and its players. Before I knew it, I was fascinated by this form of racing, and now I am all-in as a fan.

Steiner came to prominence as one of the breakout stars of the highly successful Netflix documentary series *Drive to Survive*. That series is credited with greatly increasing interest in F1 in the US. Steiner, who has been a formidable figure in motor racing for decades, is a wonderful character known for his straight talk that usually includes his trademark profanity. With the blessing of WBTV,

I made it my mission to do stories about this team and its progress over the years as it faced off with established European teams with boatloads of money, like Mercedes, Red Bull, and Ferrari.

"Our goal with this car is to score points," Steiner told me when the team introduced its first car in 2016. "First, we need to go out there and show that we can do the job, that we can finish races, that we are respected by the fans and other teams in the paddock. Then, we want to score points. That is the ultimate goal."

To do that, the team turned to veteran driver Romain Grosjean, who had driven in several European race circuits along with a stint with the Lotus F1 team and newcomer Esteban Gutiérrez.

"What Gene Haas and everyone at Haas F1 Team is building is impressive, and I'm very proud to be a part of it," Grosjean told me in an interview for WBTV. "This is a new opportunity with a new team that is taking a very different approach to Formula One. I believe in their approach, and they believe in me."

When I asked Grosjean about his impression of Kannapolis on his first visit to the area, he talked about his passion for racing and even gave a nod to a homegrown hero. "I love it, I'm passionate about racing even before being a Formula One driver," Grosjean said. "To see that all the [NASCAR] teams are in the same area and the statue of Dale Earnhardt, it's big and I really like it."

Grosjean drove for the team for several seasons with mixed results. He may be best known for dramatically crashing in the 2020 Bahrain Grand Prix, getting out of his car that was consumed in flames, and walking away. That he suffered only minor injuries and is now actively racing in the IndyCar circuit is a testament to the safety procedures put in place in F1 over the years.

One of my favorite interviews with Steiner was in the weeks prior to the famed Monaco Grand Prix in 2016. While most racing fans in the Carolinas and particularly around Concord and Kannapolis were focused on the Coca-Cola 600 at Charlotte Motor Speedway, Steiner told me he was hopeful that some of those die-hard NASCAR fans would give his team some attention too.

"Have a look at that, you know, try to look away from what you hear about it and just have a look at it and see if you're interested and try to tune yourself in. Because maybe before it wasn't interesting because there was nothing American there, now there is an American team," Steiner told me. "Just try to get interested so you have something to look at that you're interest in, if you're a fan for Haas F1, then I'm sure you will come back to look for more of that, so, give it a go, you know, forget about the past, try to look at it with a new set of eyes because a US team is there."

In some ways, it still seems like a well-kept secret that this team is located in Kannapolis. When I asked people on the street about it, few knew what I was talking about. "I think it has been a well-kept secret," Kannapolis City Manager Mike Legg told me one time. "We have to continue to talk to people about it because a lot of people don't know that it's here and the impact that it has worldwide."

Covering the team gave me the opportunity to do several interviews with Steiner and with other Haas drivers, like Kevin Magnussen, and has opened up a new interest in my life that I really enjoy. I have written a story on the WBTV website after every F1 race since 2016 to document how the team did. These were based on the press release the team would send me about an hour after the checkered flag fell, and I would add a headline and a few lines of my own after watching the race on TV. Over time, I noticed that those stories had their own following of fans, and that was gratifying. That's one aspect of the job that I miss now in retirement and is another reminder of how gracious the station was to allow me to post those stories week after week.

If any celebrity stands out to me more than the others, it has to be Richard Petty. Petty was the first sports hero I had as a kid. He, St. Louis Cardinals baseball legends Bob Gibson and Lou Brock, and Washington Redskins quarterback Billy Kilmer were at the top of my list. I wrote to Petty several times when I was a kid, and each time received a color picture of the "King" and his current car, complete with that trademark swooping, swirly signature that he has perfected.

I had the chance to meet and interview Petty several times over the years, but for me, every time was like the first. I still get excited when that opportunity comes up, and I've thrown out all pretense of being objective when I do stories about Richard Petty. One of my favorite Petty moments came during a race week at Charlotte Motor Speedway during 2007. Our station had committed me, along with one of our anchors, Jamie Boll; a producer; and two photographers to spend a week of covering events at the track. During the week prior to the race, we did all kinds of stories about the fans, the track, souvenirs, security, etc. It was the kind of assignment that I loved, especially when we put so many resources into it like we did that year.

Fans, too, spent a lot of money. Many arrived a week or two before the race in campers. Camping at the track is just as popular now as it ever was. The speedway even gives awards to the campers who arrive first and travel the longest distance. They set up in the campgrounds around the track, putting out chairs and picnic tables, flags of their favorite drivers, and even live plants and landscaping to create a homey feel. They spend time at the track watching qualifying and the special concerts and other events that lead up to the race. Many tow a small car or a trailer with motorcycles so they can leave the track for a quick run to a local restaurant or shopping area.

Usually during that kind of coverage, I have to be live for the five and six o'clock shows. I would have a different story for each one, and also occasionally appear with Jamie in the 5:30 show, just to talk about some particular issue. Jamie and I are both big fans of the sport, and that obviously helps us cover it in a more informed manner. The truth is that in Charlotte, very few news reporters know or care one whit about racing, but because it's such a big business and such a part of our culture, we must cover it.

We had fun with our stories. One day, Jamie and I and the rest of our crew actually started a grill live on the air and whipped up some barbecued chicken. Another time, I had to eat a monstrosity called the "beastly rib." Hotter than anything I've ever seen, tasted, or heard about. It burned my lips and later made a most unfriendly exit. Still, it was a blast.

On one day in 2007, I had a story for five and six and was going to talk with Jamie in the 5:30 broadcast. It was a little unusual, because Jamie didn't tell me what we were talking about. He just said it would be about "the race, competition, tires, stuff like that." *Okay, whatever you say*, I thought. At 5:45 we went live. Jamie and I were standing there, and he was saying something about how the race was shaping up, when all of a sudden I saw something out of the corner of my eye. It was a white cowboy hat, one of those big Charlie One

Horse hats, and under it, the King. The producer, Brian Stephenson, had set me up for a surprise. The whole thing was done just so Petty would walk into our live shot and present me with an official crew member shirt. I was flipping out. I was so excited that I forgot that I was a reporter and went back to being a ten-year-old fan, smiling from ear to ear, reaching out enthusiastically to shake Petty's hand, tripping over myself to tell him how happy I was to see him, all while I was on the air live and holding my microphone. Petty was saying that he had heard about "this reporter that was always talking about the Pettys," and he thought it would be better if I was actually on the team. We finished up the shot after two or three minutes. Petty stayed around to pose for pictures and sign his famous autograph a few dozen times. I get happy just thinking about that moment, and, of course, I have it all on tape.

My biggest thrill every year when I covered NASCAR at Charlotte Motor Speedway was when I first got to the track and saw Richard Petty in his team's garage stall. I walked around the garage area until I found the bay for car #43. He would be inside speaking to crew members or maybe on the roof of the trailer with a stopwatch in hand, keeping an eye on the cars circling the track. Once I found the King, I was able to get on with my work for the day.

The King and I would have another rendezvous before I retired, and it was a good one. My coworker and friend Brian Stephenson, the wizard behind the first Petty Surprise years earlier, put together something even more spectacular.

During one of my last weeks on the job, I was contacted about a story at the racetrack that would feature interviews about Speedway Children's Charities. SCC is a wonderful organization that contributes millions of dollars to nonprofits in areas where Speedway Motorsports tracks are located. I had done several stories about SCC in the past, so this didn't sound unusual to me. That morning, I did my beat checks with law enforcement and then headed to the speedway. I was met by the always bubbly and eager-to-help Samantha Waddell, who was in communications for the speedway. She met me in the lobby and said we had to wait a few minutes for the SCC folks to get here. After about fifteen minutes, she took a phone call and walked away. She ended the call, walked back over to me, and said we needed to get on the elevator to go up to The Speedway Club. The Speedway Club is a world-class restaurant located in the tower at the front of the track and is also used for some very nice functions throughout the year. In this case, it was being used to host one of the happiest moments of my career. Loaded down with camera, lights, tripod, and microphones, I walked off the elevator and started to turn the corner into the restaurant when I was immediately blinded by bright lights. I saw a TV camera, and my first thought was that I had just walked into someone else's shot and ruined their video.

I then recognized that the photographer was Corey Schmidt, my friend and coworker from WBTV. *What is he doing here?* I wondered. Then I noticed Stephenson standing with a lot of other people. I looked to my left and saw Richard Petty and Kyle Petty sitting at one of the tables set with a white linen tablecloth and glasses of water. Kyle Petty said hello, motioned for me to come over, then said, "You're not working today." I put down all of my equipment and joined them at the table. Sixty-two-year-old me suddenly became that ten-year-old fan boy all over again.

We spent the next forty minutes talking at the table with the

Pettys interviewing me! I had to keep stopping, just to make sure that I was awake and not having some wonderful dream. *Here I am, sitting at a table with Richard and Kyle Petty.* They asked me how I became a Petty fan, what were some of my favorite Petty moments, and what were some of my best memories from Charlotte Motor Speedway. I answered each question and couldn't help but cry when I told them about my dad picking me up early from school and taking me to qualifying, just so I could see that Petty-blue Plymouth #43 in person. At the end of the interview, Richard and Kyle gave me one of their signature cowboy hats.

The station put together a really fun story about our meeting, and the Petty public relations team made up some really fun social media posts. That became one of the most talked about stories I had ever been a part of, and it's something people constantly ask me about.

Many people say when they met one of their heroes in person they were disappointed, but I can tell you that in the case of Richard and Kyle Petty, they're sincere and genuine people. That family is an absolute treasure. They were everything I hoped they would be when I was a boy listening to NASCAR races on the radio on Sunday afternoon with my dad.

Oh, and Kyle's remark about me not having to work that day didn't carry any weight with the news director. As soon as my Petty Surprise was over, I was back on the clock and on the way to turn in my story for the day.

13: Celebrities

I had the pleasure of interviewing movie star Andie MacDowell twice and she was very gracious. This is Andie with me and friend and former coworker Jim Travers who worked as my photographer for the second interview.

MANY ASSUME THAT THE TV LIFE IS glamorous and that reporters are treated as quasi-celebrities. There's some truth in that, but more often it's a day-to-day toil where you work for ten to twelve hours to be on TV for two minutes. The job does let you dip into a more glamorous world occasionally. Along with the sports celebrities I've interviewed, there have been quite a few other famous faces who stood before my lens, from presidents to pop stars to posers.

I've met, or at least been in the same room with, five presidents. My first experience came during my radio career when I met former President Gerald Ford at the Crosby Golf Tournament at the Bermuda Run Country Club near Winston-Salem in the early nineties. Maybe he had a bad round of golf or maybe it was hot, but he wasn't in a particularly good mood. He walked through the media tent, which was set up as you exited the club, very quickly, without a word for anyone. That was a disappointment, since as a child I really admired Ford for his attempt to bring dignity back to the White House in the wake of the Watergate scandal.

President George H.W. Bush, on the other hand, was friendly, funny, and completely cordial. I met him when he came to visit the small Rowan County town of Faith during the 1992 election season. Faith is known for having a large Fourth of July celebration, including a parade that draws tens of thousands of revelers. President Bush came to town to take part in a softball game and a picnic. I was fortunate enough to have been chosen to be the public address announcer and official scorer for the ball game. Bush had played college baseball at Yale and was eager for this chance to be back on the field. What a thrill it was to announce him coming up to the plate as George "Pappy" Bush, his college nickname. Bush was no slouch with the stick, slapping a pitch back into the hole between second and third. He ran to first and was safe. Technically, he reached first on a fielder's choice, but I scored him with a base hit. I figured he was the president, I was the official scorer, and the game didn't mean anything anyway, so it's a hit. After the game, Bush stood near the pitcher's mound and signed dozens of autographs. I still have the score book from the game that he signed with a thick black marker.

I saw President Clinton in Norfolk, Virginia, at the Navy base. The occasion was the memorial service for Lakeina Francis, who was a sailor on board the USS Cole that was attacked by terrorists in Yemen. Francis died in the bomb blast that ripped a large hole in the side of the destroyer. She was from the Woodleaf community in Rowan County. Her parents were some of the kindest and most gracious people I've ever met. Lakeina and the other victims of the attack were warmly remembered by President Clinton. Watching him make his remarks made me appreciate what an effective speaker Clinton was during his time in the White House. I would later talk with him in Salisbury when he visited as part of his wife Hillary's presidential campaign.

I had the chance to see George W. Bush on more than one occasion, as he came many times to North Carolina during his eight years in the White House. His first trip was shortly after his election, when he visited a middle school in Concord. That's where I came so close to getting a one-on-one interview with him.

His visit was in a school gym that had been rearranged to hold a large number of people and to give the media a good working area. My photographer and I arrived early, since the Secret Service insisted on it. We went through all the usual checks and inspections of the equipment and found our spot in what I thought would be a good vantage point. We had a good view of the stage, but we were right on the corner of the cordoned off area, and I had a hunch that if he walked out into the crowd, he might come our way. I was right.

We were live on the air during our noon show. The president had just wrapped his remarks and was working the crowd, coming right toward us. He kept inching closer, and I just knew we were going to get him. He leaned in right next to me to say hello to a well-known local philanthropist and, as he backed out, I shouted, "Mr. President!" He looked right at me and just as I leaned in to try to ask him a quick question, a crew from CNN pushed right between us, with the reporter shouting at him to comment about some international incident that was a big deal for a few hours that day. The moment was lost, Bush leaned back, didn't answer the question, and kept walking without saying a word. I was disappointed, but still was on live TV.

Congressman Robin Hayes was walking behind President Bush, and I grabbed him and we did a short question and answer. I asked him if he would go get Bush and bring him back. Robin laughed, then walked straight over to him and started whispering in his ear. Bush turned and looked back, but again, the CNN crew was still yelling at him, pushing us almost to the floor. The president appeared to be considering coming over to my spot, but as the CNN reporter shouted another question at him, he turned and walked on. For years it's been a running joke that anytime I see Robin Hayes, he assures me he is still trying to get me an interview with George W. Bush.

A couple years later, President Bush visited Charlotte, and I was chosen to be the local pool photographer for the visit. That means I was the only one allowed to travel with him and shoot his activities, and then our station had to make copies of all the video for any other local station that wanted it. I was honored. Bush said hello to me, but didn't do any one-on-one interviews that day. Still, it was amazing to travel in a presidential motorcade, blowing through stop lights at high speed and seeing both supporters and protestors lining the streets.

Jimmy Carter was present with the others at the funeral of Reverend Billy Graham, which I was covering. He kept to himself and didn't seem to really associate with the others, especially his fellow democrat Bill Clinton.

In covering campaigns, I've been with Hillary Clinton, Pat

Buchanan, Bob Dole, John Edwards, Dan Quayle, and Senator Elizabeth Dole, who I covered extensively since she is a native of Salisbury and attended the same high school that I did. Senator Dole was kind enough to allow videographer Brian Stephenson and I into her office for an interview on the day of President Reagan's funeral in Washington, DC. That was the same day that Brian and I ran into Senator John McCain outside. We asked him for an interview, but he deferred, saying he had to get inside for an interview with *Good Morning America*. He also said he would come back to that same spot in about fifteen minutes and would speak with us. Then he got into the car and left. We debated on what we should do. Neither of us really thought he would come back, but that's exactly what he did, and he gave us a great interview.

The Reagan funeral was an experience that I will always treasure. Brian and I needed to find people from the Charlotte area and across the Carolinas who were coming and waiting in the long line of mourners wanting to pay their respects. The line led to the Capitol rotunda, where the president was lying in state. We walked along the line, and I held my mic with the WBTV mic flag. People who recognized me or the station logo would call out to us and were usually up for doing a short interview while they waited. The organizers of the funeral did set up a special media gallery that allowed credentialed media to bypass the line and get inside the rotunda for about eight minutes. This gave us the chance to get our video and then get out of the way of the next crew. Brian and I noticed a man in a full Native American outfit, complete with an elaborate headdress. There were police officers stationed around the coffin to make sure the people kept moving, but when this man approached, they made an exception. He was carrying a long feather. As he walked around the four points of the coffin, he stopped and held the feather out and then bowed and prayed. No one seemed to mind. Later, we saw President Reagan's wife Nancy and other members of the family in the limousines driving through Washington.

The most surprising interviews I've done were with people that intimidated me. Reverend Jesse Jackson was a lot taller in person than I had realized. He was one of the first nationally known figures I ever interviewed, and I wanted to get the story right and not sound like an idiot compared to the national journalists he dealt with every day. I met him twice. Once at a historically black college that was having serious money problems; he was there to bring attention to the school and help to raise funds. Jackson was warm and friendly and very easy to speak with.

Now that I've gone through the politicians, the funniest interview had to be with television star Mr. T, who was appearing in the Mooresville Christmas Parade. His signature show *The A-Team* was playing on the TV Land channel, and the local cable company arranged the appearance. I had to interview him while I walked with my camera beside his moving convertible in the parade, and every few minutes, no matter what he was talking about, he would stop and yell out, "I pity the fool!" and, "Did anybody bring me a sandwich?"

Several years later, I got to interview a few of the stars of the animated movie *Cars* after a critic's screening of the movie at Charlotte Motor Speedway. Larry the Cable Guy was funny, telling me that I was too stiff by wearing a coat and tie and that next time we should do the interview in "our underwear."

Cheech Marin, John Ratzenberger, Richard Petty, and Bonnie

Hunt were all on the line-up as well. The reporter who spoke with Bonnie Hunt just before me was apparently a pretty good-looking guy. We passed each other in the room as he was leaving. Hunt was making purring noises and looking at her assistant like she was somewhat impressed by this guy by giving a wink and an eye roll. So I thought, *Oh yeah, now she's going to see me and start laughing after being interviewed by Dash Riprock and now answering questions from Gilligan.* I took my seat on the stool across from her and introduced myself. She never made eye contact, she just looked at her assistant again and said something like "Whew." That was the only interview I actually finished up before the allotted time ran out. She was mentally done for the day, and I could tell. I asked her a couple things, she gave me some standard answers, and I just thanked her for her time.

I've seen her since on other shows and I think she's really funny and engaging, but that day I think she was ready to wrap it up after speaking with at least a dozen reporters.

Paul Newman voiced a critical part in the movie, the character "Doc." I and about two dozen other reporters got to talk to him at Charlotte Motor Speedway, then go with him out on the track where he got into a vintage Hudson Hornet painted up to resemble his movie character. Newman put on the driver's suit and helmet, climbed into the car, and took a few laps around the oval. He was a class act all the way.

One of my favorite celebrities that I've met has to be the beautiful Andie MacDowell. Not only is she stunning, but she is wonderfully friendly and has a great memory. I first met her at a reception in Asheville at Grove Park Inn for Ruth Bell Graham, the wife of

Billy Graham. MacDowell was involved in charity work and lived in Asheville. There was a small press reception before the main event, and she was one of those people who has so much beauty and charm you stop in your tracks when you first see her. At least I did. She sat with Graham's daughter Ann and the bestselling author Patricia Cornwell, answering questions from reporters. For some reason, the idea hit me to see if, by any chance, Andie would join me for my live shot at 11:07 that night, about an hour after the end of the gala. I figured that it couldn't hurt to ask, and all she could do was say no. I wrote out my request and gave it to her assistant. To my utter amazement, fifteen minutes later the assistant told me that Andie would be delighted to agree with my request.

I worked through writing my story, trying to make sure that the focus stayed on Ruth Bell Graham and not Andie MacDowell. At around nine thirty, MacDowell's assistant came looking for me. She told me Andie was going to have to leave early and couldn't stay until eleven. At first I was sorely disappointed until the assistant suggested she go get Andie and we could record what we had planned to live. Brilliant! *Yes, go get her now!*

Five minutes later, Andie was standing next to me for the interview. She was so easygoing about it all that she even taped a silly little skit with me to use on our *Football Friday Night* show where we joked about having watched the game together.

I was now her biggest fan, but it got better. Two years later, she was in Charlotte to promote a television movie in which she was starring. She had scheduled media interviews in Charlotte because the movie was going to be debuted in a Charlotte theater before being on TV. The station asked me to do the interview, knowing how "close" the two of us were. Again, to my surprise, when I got to the home where she was doing the interviews, she saw me, her eyes lit up, and she said, "Oh, I remember you, hey!" I was completely beguiled and in disbelief. So, using my innate charm and verbal repartee, I replied, "Really?" We had a wonderful chat and a good interview, and again, we recorded another skit to use on *Football Friday Night*.

After the interview, she posed for a picture with my photographer and me. As I left, we joked about when we will see each other again. I'm sure it will happen someday!

Some other notables have included interviewing singer and former soap opera star Rick Springfield in his motel room on July 4 prior to a concert and talking with singer Demi Lovato about the pressures of being a role model. That interview took place when she was the unlikely star at the grand opening of a new Verizon phone store. I very much enjoyed doing an interview with Roger McGuinn of the Byrds on the campus of Catawba College. He actually played a bit of "Turn, Turn, Turn," while I was getting video of him tuning a guitar. My childhood favorites, The Monkees, did an interview at a Best Buy store in Charlotte. Well, three of them. Mike Nesmith was not part of that tour, but Micky, Davy, and Peter were very nice.

Wayne Newton was a scream, giving an energetic interview and then really camping it up for yet another *Football Friday Night* skit. I met him at the same time I met country singer Trace Adkins. Both were performing at a special concert at Charlotte Motor Speedway. Adkins was pretty funny, very warm, and didn't seem to care that I had no idea who he was or what he sang.

I was able to meet several stars from my childhood. I had a great time with Jerry "The Beaver" Mathers in Kannapolis while he was promoting prescription drug assistance for poor and uninsured patients and health awareness at the Cabarrus County Health Department. One of the actors who occasionally shared the screen with Mathers on *Leave It to Beaver* and a lot of other 1960s shows was a guy named "TV" Tommy Ivo. He was at the zMAX Dragway during a running of the NHRA Four Wide Nationals. After his acting career, he was also a drag racer of note and built a special drag car that had four engines. He was a lot of fun to be around and really seemed to enjoy working on the story with me.

In Mount Airy, I had the privilege of meeting Betty Lynn several times. She played Barney's girlfriend Thelma Lou on *The Andy Griffith Show*. She was one of the nicest and most gracious people I've ever spoken to. During one visit to the Andy Griffith Museum, I also met Donna Douglas, who played Elly May from *The Beverly Hillbillies*. She and Betty Lynn were signing autographs for fans, and the line stretched through the museum and out the front door. Even so, both took the time to spend a few minutes with me doing interviews and talking about their careers and the lasting adoration being shown by the fans.

I managed to get a laugh out of George Clooney when he was promoting the 2008 movie *Leatherheads*. Set in the 1920s, parts of the movie were shot in Salisbury, so he and Renee Zellwegger held a press conference in costume at the historic Salisbury train station before the film's release. During the Q and A, I asked him how he liked working in an authentic railroad station in our town and if he had any parts for a "dashing middle-aged reporter" type. He laughed and responded that if I knew any "dashing middle-aged reporters," then I should let him know. I had actually seen Clooney, briefly, while the movie was being shot at that train station that still looks like something from the pre-Depression era. One morning, I wanted to try to get some video of the filming going on. It was raining hard that day. I covered my camera and headed to the train station. The nearby parking lot was filled with the trailers and catering trucks that follow the movies from location to location. I went right to the front of the station, joined by another reporter with a competing station. As expected, the police and the movie people stopped us cold right on the street. It was all they could do to at least let us stand under the overhang and not out in the rain.

A woman who handled such matters immediately began telling us every reason why we weren't allowed to stand on the public street and public sidewalk. The police officers who were standing there were friends of mine, though, and they knew the law, so at that point they actually intervened and told the feisty woman that technically, we were certainly allowed to stand right where we were. Still incensed, she backed down, but told us we could come no further and if we disrupted the filming, *blah blah blah*. Feeling newly strengthened by the aid of Salisbury's finest, I asked if we could get a shot of Clooney or Zellwegger. "No!" was the curt reply. The other reporter started to argue a bit, and I just let him go.

While they spoke, I noticed three men, covered head to toe in rain gear, walking out from the parking lot and toward the entrance to the station. I lifted my camera to my shoulder and started shoot-ing. The other reporter saw what I was doing and did the same thing. We couldn't see the faces of the men, except for a small hole that revealed the eyes, nose, and mouth. Just as they walked right by us, one of the men said, "Hey guys, how you doing?" Yeah, it was George

Clooney. He flashed a smile, ducked out of the rain, and went inside. The movie protector woman was dumbfounded, and the police were laughing. The other reporter and I were so busy getting that shot we didn't even think to ask him anything.

Later in the day, we were able to get more shots by going around to the back side of the train station. From that vantage point, we saw Clooney in the director's chair. Again, the movie tyrant tried to have us removed, but again, the old problem of us being on public property kept us in our spots. Not to be outdone, she was able to get two boxcars moved down the railroad track several hundred yards and right in between us and the movie set. Of course, we had so much video by that time, it didn't really matter.

I'm still waiting for Clooney to call about that part for the dashing middle-aged-okay-now-senior reporter.

There are two celebrities that I tried, unsuccessfully, to interview several times. My colleague and mentor, legendary reporter and documentary maker Steve Crump, managed to snag a one-on-one interview with Paul McCartney after a concert in Charlotte. Crump told me it was only because someone had tipped him off to "the right place to be standing" when McCartney came off the stage. The tip was solid, and Sir Paul spent a few minutes with Steve that night. I tried on several occasions to find that right spot and even wrote repeatedly to McCartney's press people to request an interview. The closest I came was getting a wave from him as he was in the back seat of a big Suburban taking him into a concert venue.

My other white whale is Ringo Starr. I wrote to his people while he was on tour with stops in the Carolinas, but was not able to come up with any success. I do understand their rationale—why would celebrities at their level feel the need to do an interview with some boob from a local station? Still, those are the two that eluded me. So, Paul, Ringo, maybe Mick Jagger . . . if you happen to see this, can we still work something out?

14: The Millwork Fire

Photo credit: The Salisbury Post

"Structure fire, 1820 South Martin Luther King Jr.," the emergency services radios blared on Friday, March 7, 2008.

I ALMOST DIDN'T GO.

I was at my usual Friday morning prayer breakfast at the Checkered Flag restaurant in Salisbury. Three friends and I meet every week, enjoying each other's company, and then we pray out loud together for specific needs. The people in the other booths think we're nuts, but such is the way of the Christian walk. Someone called to tell me there was a fire at Salisbury Millworks. I thought it was probably not a big deal. The Salisbury Fire Department was already on scene, and that usually meant no matter how close I was, the fire was going to be extinguished before I could get to it. Even so, something told me to go. I can't describe it, but I apologized to my friends and left.

I got to the fire in just a couple of minutes and drove to the front entrance of the plant behind one of the fire trucks. An employee was in the driveway, and when he saw my media vehicle, he told me that I needed to leave and that I couldn't come onto the property. My vehicle was a white Ford Explorer with the large WBTV logo on the sides. It was easy to spot and, most of the time, that was a good thing. People would usually wave or say hello, but often in breaking-news situations, it meant I couldn't get where I wanted to go because sometimes the media is not welcome. As it turned out, leaving the front and going to the back afforded me a much better position to see what was going on.

I was the first reporter on the scene and the only one for quite a while. It was raining heavily, and it was cold. I put on my cumbersome rain gear, jumped out, grabbed the camera from the back of my SUV, put the camera on the tripod, and started shooting video. Initially, from the eye of a news photographer, it wasn't an astounding sight. Smoke was coming out of some windows in what appeared to be a small office building. I exchanged good mornings with police officer Andy Efird and rookie officer Andy Carlton. I nodded at some of the firefighters who were going about their work in their usual professional manner. I called the WBTV assignment desk and told them where I was, that I was covering a fire, probably not a big deal, and I'd stay a few more minutes and run to the bureau on the square in downtown Salisbury and feed in some video for noon news.

I can't really put my finger on when it hit me, but something about this call had changed. The police had allowed me to cross the railroad tracks and get some closer images. But instead of the fire getting smaller, it appeared to me that it was growing. The smoke coming from the building was heavier and darker.

"The smoke continues to grow, lying low and blowing around all over the place, rough as I've ever seen it to be the exterior of a fire. We were wearing our hoods over our mouth and nose to try and filter some of the smoke. It began to look like the defensive attack was doing some good. Then we heard a 'Mayday' from Quint 4 [Quint 4 was the name of the fire truck] that he had fire all around him and it was hot," wrote Salisbury firefighter and close personal friend Jay Baker. His journal, written shortly after the fire, provides a fascinating eyewitness account of the events of that day.

There was a bright-orange glow in the window that I believe was in owner Norde Wilson's office. I interviewed Wilson a few minutes later, and he was still confident that the fire would be extinguished quickly and gave high praise for the work of the Salisbury Fire Department. His only regret, at that point, was that some fine cherry woodwork in his office was probably being destroyed. Then there was another significant change. The smoke was mixed with flames coming from the roof of the office, flames mixed with smoke now pouring out of Wilson's office window. There was more smoke coming from eaves and doorways, loading dock doors and windows, coming from the huge manufacturing area that ran nearly a block long. Soon the flames overpowered the smoke—bright, orange, fierce flames, fueled by superheated air, crawled on every surface.

"The conditions are terrible, and we don't have but a few minutes before collapse is inevitable," Baker wrote.

I zoomed in with my camera on a specific spot in which I saw a bright-blue flame near the front of the building. A firefighter later told me it was probably one of the chemicals used in the plant. The flames became so big they leapt into the air over the brick building now struggling to stay standing.

Then another, haunting change.

No one told me that any of the dozens of firefighters on the scene had been hurt, and I didn't hear the "Mayday" call from Captain

Barkley, but I didn't need to. You could see it on their faces. I knew something had happened, and that it was horrible.

Salisbury Fire Chief Robert Parnell walked by with a look of shock and sadness. I called the station and said they'd better send me some help because I knew now this was not just a structure fire like I'd seen hundreds of times before in my career. An ambulance moved in close to the building, surprisingly near the flames. Chief Parnell walked by again and asked me and the other news crews if we would hold off reporting anything "until families could be notified." Those words made it pretty clear to me that at least one firefighter was hurt and that it was serious.

Two years earlier, to help me with a story, Chief Parnell had dressed me up in firefighter's turnout gear and let me go into an apartment that firefighters were burning for training. I can still feel the heat from that day. As I crawled on the floor in that heavy gear, awkwardly trying to carry my camera, I wondered how firefighters could do this and still keep their senses. There was a point, probably just a minute or two into it, that the firefighters started to pull me out. I wasn't ready to go, but when I saw a part of plastic on the cover of my camera melting, I didn't need any more convincing.

But this was no training fire; this was a raging inferno that had claimed victims.

We later learned that Salisbury firefighters Vic Isler, forty, and Justin Monroe, nineteen, died while fighting the fire. Justin Monroe began his firefighting career at the age of sixteen as a junior firefighter with the Millers Ferry Fire Department, and was currently serving as lieutenant with the department. Victor Isler had come to Salisbury from the New York Fire Department EMS in 2007 and had worked at Ground Zero following the attacks on the World Trade Center on September 11, 2001.

Firefighter Baker wrote, "During this Mr. Treme [Salisbury City Manager] must have gotten word, he's wandering around, then comes toward us, close to the collapse area. I put my arm around him and walk him back out. He asked, 'How many have we lost?' I told him, 'Two, I think. This is our worst day.' We hugged and cried together briefly. I then began to hug and cry with everyone left. The building is now an afterthought, everyone is out, let it burn. The inside of the building was like a bomb had dropped on it, or a war zone."

Captain Rick Barkley was the firefighter who made that Mayday call. Fighting the fire with Isler and Monroe, Barkley was seriously injured and had to be rescued by a rapid intervention team. A firewall in the building collapsed just as Jay Baker had predicted, trapping the men inside. Barkley was side by side with Isler and Monroe, but somehow survived the fire, in part by finding a gash in the fire hose, pulling it close to his body, and allowing the water to surround him.

"The pain stopped from the burns, I guess my body shut down, I can't explain it. I was hurting and then the pain stopped," Barkley told me in an interview two years after the fire. "A kind of like a peace came about and I'm thinking, I'm lying on the hose. I'm either going to burn to death or the place is going to fall down on top of me, but I was all right with that."

One truly telling point about the character of these men and women in the fire service was that once they found out that they had lost two colleagues, they didn't stop fighting this fire. There were one or two who took a few seconds to hug, but then they charged right back in. The grief and the pain had to be put aside while the flames continued to ensnare the building. I watched as an employee's car was overcome and then consumed in seconds by the fire, leaving only a charred and smoking black frame. I kept shooting video even though the heat was so intense that I had to retreat. I still had a job to do; I had a story to tell.

The station did send two other photographers to help me, and we spent the rest of the day on the scene. I had to do three live reports during our noon news, plus one at five, one at six, one at seven, and an additional story for WFMY in Greensboro and WRAL in Raleigh. My video, those unbelievable images, went out to CBS News in New York and to CBS and affiliated stations across the world.

I cried at the end of my five o'clock live shot. I couldn't help it. This was my hometown. These were people I knew and respected, and they were hurting, so I was hurting. It may not have been professional, but it was real. I said something to the effect that in my sixteen years of covering news on television, this was the worst, the bottom-line worst story I had ever covered. I've seen a lot of bad things—suffering, anger—but this was the nadir of all of it.

That pain led me to do some things out of character for me. I snapped at several people in our newsroom, including our anchor, Maureen O'Boyle. I snapped at good people at Rowan Regional Medical Center. I snapped at my wife. I knew I had to get my temperament under control. I prayed for peace for myself, but then felt guilty asking God for anything when so many people needed so much more than I did.

The next few days were a blur of events and images, some sad and heartbreaking, some hopeful and wonderful. The show of support from the community was truly encouraging. Banners, ribbons, signs—all offered prayers to the families of the fallen firefighters and for those still on the job. As a reporter, it was good to have some positive things to say about the horror that I had seen on Friday, but there were difficult and awkward moments too. As always, some of my cohorts in the media didn't want to respect what I felt were reasonable rules for covering the aftermath of such tragedies. Going around barricades, running to try to interview people leaving the service when they've been told that was off limits were two examples of this behavior. And as is often the case, the one television station that had repeatedly reported inaccurate information on the day of the fire and had virtually no ties to this community was rewarded for their aggressive efforts. But I just didn't think this was the time to be concerned with beating the competition.

I reported on how firefighters from neighboring cities were covering calls for Salisbury and Rowan County to allow time for our local firefighters to grieve and to take part in the memorial services. I talked to Brad Jordan, a firefighter who was there the day of the Millwork fire and who had seen death before when he was riding with firefighter Jim Shue of the Locke Fire Department twelve years earlier and was involved in an accident in the fire truck that took Shue's life. Yet there was Jordan, married to a firefighter, and ready to run to the next call.

For days, there was behind-the-scenes drama about how the media would be allowed to cover the day of the funeral. I wanted to have my camera there, and I was willing to "pool" the video and share it with every other station. I knew this was a historic event and that it should be documented, but my perspective on it was that it should not overrule the wishes of two families when it came to media coverage as they were dealing with their immense grief. The family did approve the request, but again, there was more drama involving other media members that lasted right up until the morning of the service.

We in the media usually play nice together, from television to print and radio, but there are times that one outlet or another has to push the bounds of reason and sensitivity. In the end it worked out, and the television camera in the chapel made it possible for the overflow crowd in Keppel Auditorium to still see and hear the images of a moving and emotional service.

Outside of the beautiful Omwake-Dearborn Chapel at Catawba College, where the service was held to accommodate the large crowd, there was a little more media drama, and even some light comedy. The media staging area was down Oliver's Way, a beautiful walkway that runs from the chapel to the auditorium on the college campus. The only problem was that the camera crews were placed in a spot behind a small weeping willow tree that greatly blocked the view. Deputy Chief Steve Whitley of the Salisbury Police Department had agreed to that camera and staging position, only after much begging on our part, and was serious about any violations of the ground rules. I mean so serious that he called the magistrate and the judge Thursday morning to give them a heads up that he may be bringing some media types to court if they crossed the line. I loved Chief Whitley. There's just enough of an edge to him that you know he's serious, but he was also realistic and willing to seek compromise, as long as it respected the wishes of the family. We joked about the tree maybe falling prey to an unknown lumberjack or beaver, but to our amazement and pleasure, Catawba officials simply dug it up and moved it. It was a major and unexpected concession, and one that was truly appreciated.

On the other hand, there was the presence of the news helicopters. Those choppers, my station's Sky 3, WSOC's Chopper 9, and WCNC's Air Star, were a vital part of broadcast news gathering, but they can be loud and intrusive. The stations were given two conflicting rules on chopper access, and when that is the case, you always go by the one that allows the most access. Lieutenant Rory Collins of the Salisbury Police Department first noticed the *wop wop wop* of the "birds," and started telling the station representatives on the ground to have the choppers back off a few miles. They did, and with the amazing technology of the zoom lens, they were still able to provide gripping images of the procession from the chapel to the nearby cemetery, along with the traditional rituals normally observed with the funeral of a firefighter.

Following the funeral, the focus turned to the investigation. What happened? Were there things that could be improved to prevent such a tragedy from happening again? A federal report conducted by the National Institute for Occupational Safety and Health was released in October 2009. The report included recommendations such as establishing and improving communication for firefighters and command staff, limiting risk to firefighters, and developing and following a plan. The report also noted that during the fire, more than 10 percent of radio transmissions between firefighters inside the building and those working outside were cut off, while 30 percent could not be understood. As a result, the City of Salisbury bought new radio systems built to tough military standards that are designed to work in actual fire conditions, such as those that unfolded at the Salisbury Millwork incident.

The focus in the community since that day has been to remember the sacrifices that were made. Every year since the fire, the city has held a special memorial service on March 7 to honor the memory of firefighters Monroe and Isler and to pay tribute to all those who choose a life of public service. Few in the community have forgotten the fire and the sacrifice made by Monroe and Isler.

"My son was such a humble person," said Lisa Monroe, the mother of Justin Monroe. "He would be amazed, so for these two families to be honored, it's truly a blessing, we thank everybody." Lisa Monroe says her son had always wanted to be a firefighter, and he was considered a rising star. "He loved it, he lived it, he breathed it, it was the most important thing in his life besides hunting and fishing."

Chief Parnell said, "The loss of Justin and Vic hurt their families and hurt the fire department family and hurt the community very deeply. They made such a sacrifice, and the community responded in such a tremendous way."

On Sunday, March 7, 2021, a new Salisbury fire station was dedicated in honor of Monroe and Isler. The Justin Monroe and Vic Isler Fire Station 6 and Training Center houses a training wing, the hazmat team, and the fire operations staff. I was greatly honored to provide the keynote address during the dedication ceremony. Citing a text from the Book of Ecclesiastes in the King James Version of the Bible, I noted that by naming the station in their honor, "Their names liveth forevermore."

The day of the fire was the worst day of my professional career. It led me to seek professional counseling for the first time and made me realize that this job could have a profound impact on my emotions and character. In the days following the fire, I wrote down my thoughts and experiences of that day and the days that followed. I found that writing could be very therapeutic. I wanted to remember these images and the feelings I experienced during this mournful time. I prayed hard that week, for the Islers and the Monroes, for Chief Parnell, Captain Barkley, our Salisbury city public information officer Karen Wilkinson, who was suffering in her own way as the cousin of Justin Monroe. I also prayed for myself, and I asked others to help me with that effort. I wanted to conduct myself first as a Christian who loves his neighbors and wants to be respectful of the sensitivity of this moment, then secondly as a compassionate reporter who still had a job to do. One of the speakers at the funeral said that God can bring that which is good out of that which is tragic. I know he can, as I certainly was an eyewitness to that during that terrible week, seeing both the tragic that we leave behind and the good that drives us to hope through the grace of God.

15: OD

Emergency responders worked to save two people who had overdosed in their pickup truck in downtown Salisbury.

SOMETIMES YOU HAVE TO BREAK THE RULES.

Throughout my career of working at crime scenes and disasters, I was always good about staying on my side of the yellow tape and not interfering with investigators. If I needed to see something more closely, I had a zoom lens. There were times where my competitors would look for a way around the tape by going around the back side of the crime scene, but that was never my style. My feeling was that while my job was important, the work of the investigators was more important, and I would still get what I needed to present a full story anyway. But on one occasion, I felt so strongly that I needed to show the true impact of a life-and-death situation that I jumped right into it.

In 2017, North Carolina experienced a sharp rise in the number of drug overdose cases. According to the North Carolina Department of Justice, there was a 32 percent increase in deaths caused by opioid overdose from the previous year. The area that I covered followed the state pattern, and overdose calls for first responders became a routine and exhausting part of their day. Emergency medical responders, firefighters, and police rush to get to overdose patients that can hopefully be brought back to life using Narcan to reverse the effects of the overdose. Many times, though, it would be too late, and the result was death. These overdoses would often occur at gas stations, fast-food restaurants, and convenience store bathrooms, as well as at private homes and apartments. Local health officials scrambled to get the word out and warn people about the dangers of opioid abuse, but the numbers continued to climb.

We did many stories on the rash of overdose cases, but rarely showed the graphic picture of what that scene looks like. We reported numbers, statistics, advice, but didn't show the frightening reality of what first responders and family members had to face every day. I had the personal conviction that I wasn't doing enough to inform my audience and thought there had to be a better way. What I wanted to do was get to the scene of a reported overdose before the first responders did so that I could show the startling images in full color, high definition. That summer I got my chance.

On Friday afternoon, August 11, 2017, I was sitting in my office finishing up the editing on the story I was presenting that day. As usual, I had the police scanner turned on in the background so that I could hear any calls about major incidents. The tones on the scanner soon sounded, and I heard the telecommunicator dispatch police, fire, and emergency medical services to an overdose involving two victims less than a block from my office. I ran out the front door, got my gear from the car, and sprinted to the 100 block of South Main Street. The skies were gray and a light rain was falling. I was there within a minute, just as the first fire truck was turning the corner. There, in front of a toy store and candy store, were two young adults lying on the wet sidewalk, both unconscious. A few bystanders were there, unsure of what to do. I started shooting video.

The young woman was pretty, with long, platinum-blonde hair, wearing a skirt. A bystander found her hanging halfway out of the passenger door of her then boyfriend's Ram truck. The bystander thought she was dead. When I arrived, she was on the ground. Her boyfriend was also unconscious on the sidewalk.

Firefighters and paramedics scrambled to do what they could to revive the two. This is where I decided I was going to move. I wouldn't be in the way, but I was going to record every bit of what was happening so that people could see something besides statistics and worried officials giving formal interviews. Shon Barnes, then serving as the Deputy Police Chief in Salisbury, made eye contact with me. I thought he was going to tell me to move back, but he didn't. I like to think he understood that, this time, I wasn't going anywhere.

Firefighters quickly surrounded the two. It took only seconds for the Narcan to take effect and bring the two back to consciousness. Bystanders told police how they found the young couple . . . and the child. Child? I looked around. There was a five-year-old boy with them, the son of the young woman. That child had been scooped up by one of the shop owners and taken inside. Minutes later Salisbury Police Captain Melonie Thompson walked quickly out of the store with the boy in her arms. He was crying, and I heard him ask, "Where are they?"

Emergency responders lifted the shirtless young man from the sidewalk and placed him on a stretcher. As he became aware of what was going on, he began arguing with them. He insisted that he was fine now and didn't want to go to the hospital. The young woman was on her feet, asking about her son and saying she didn't want to go to the hospital either. I walked over to the truck. Both doors were open, and I shot video of what I saw in the driver's seat, including some change, a phone card, a small plastic tube that police said could be used as a pipe, and a small plastic bag. A pocketbook rested in the passenger seat. A lanyard with keys and a skateboard lay on the ground just below the door.

Within a few minutes, the scene was cleared. The two people were gone, and the child was placed with a family member. Bystanders moved along, and shopkeepers swept the sidewalk. I called the station and told them what had happened and what I wanted to do with this story. I wanted to show all of it. I wanted to show the faces of these two young adults and the faces of the first responders who had just saved their lives. I wanted to show the faces of the bystanders looking on. I reported this story as an eyewitness, not a reporter. My producer agreed and even gave me a little more time than usual for this story. The impact from the television story and the post on Facebook was immediate and huge and covered a wide range of reactions. Most viewers appreciated the story and said it needed to be told; others were upset at the images presented and said we were wrong and shouldn't have shown such graphic footage of people passed out on the sidewalk. Still others couldn't wait to chime in with comments that mocked the two people and indicated that overdose deaths were beneficial because it was a good way to "thin the herd."

"I have no sympathy for the addicts," one man wrote. "They

hurt everyone around them, including children. All these selfish bastards think about is themselves. No one else. No sympathy." He also described my story as "media sensationalism."

"I'm going to say it, let them die," wrote a woman on the WBTV Facebook page. "Let their children go to relatives afterward, or foster care."

Many more did express sympathy, though, and encouraged the community to pray for those addicted to drugs. A very few asked about services available to help with the escalating situation.

Weeks later, the young woman who had overdosed reached out to me and said she wanted to tell her side of the story, adding that she believed it would help people.

Six weeks after she'd been found hanging lifelessly out of a pickup truck cab, the young woman sat with me in a coffee shop just a few blocks from where the incident took place. She was well dressed and professional in appearance, a stark contrast to our first "meeting." She admitted that in the days following the overdose and the media coverage, I was the one person in the world she hated more than any other. I expected that, but so be it. That's when she said something that surprised me: "The way it happened is turning out to be a really good thing," she said.

"We got a 'point,' which is an amount of powder about as big as a pencil eraser and we split it and we snorted it," the young woman told me.

There were parts of the day that she didn't remember. "I remember him parking the truck, cutting it off, and opening his door, and there wasn't even a moment of something doesn't feel right, it was just gone. I wake up, I was on the sidewalk, it's instantaneous and I knew, I opened my eyes, I knew what just happened, I knew what I did."

She also realized what it could have cost her. "I finally realized, I mean, I made the mistake that all addicts make. I thought I had control of it, and I didn't. That day I realized it was out of control, I hurt my son . . . my son is my life, my world," she said.

She was now being treated for her drug addiction and vowing to stay clean. She returned to the 100 block of South Main Street one afternoon to take a picture of herself, looking healthy and happy. She used that picture in a Facebook post that was shared thousands of times. She told me she didn't want to be remembered as the girl who OD'd on the sidewalk. "I really like the feeling I get from knowing that I'm helping somebody. By helping other people, I think it's helping me," she said. "I didn't want to go back on the news, I didn't want to be on the news to begin with, but since I was already there, may as well give somebody something better to remember me by than just the girl dead in the truck."

I haven't spoken to her in several years and don't know anything else about her progress since then. I hope and have prayed that she has been able to recover, and I'm thankful that she came to an understanding of how her example could be used to help others.

The overdoses in the community didn't go away as a result of my story, but I know it created significant awareness. Local health officials from several counties used the video in their training and in community meetings. Rowan County continued to struggle with large numbers of cases. According to the North Carolina Department of Health and Human Services, the rate of opioid overdose deaths per 100,000 North Carolina residents between 2017 and 2021 was 38.9 in Rowan County, 22.7 statewide. The now widespread availability of Narcan has reduced the number of overdose deaths, thankfully. The product is dispensed free of charge from local health and public safety agencies, and from a vending machine right outside the detention center.

"We want to connect with our citizens. We want to make sure that they are here tomorrow so that they can get to rehabilitation, and we can get them help, but if we don't have that lifesaving drug of Narcan, we're not going to see that happen," Alyssa Harris, Rowan County's director of public health, told me in September 2023.

This story has stuck with me over the years. If I had not been willing to push harder and get in closer on that day, the story would not have had the impact that it did. I could have just stayed in my office and finished my other story. The overdose scene would have cleared within twenty minutes and then be forgotten. I could have covered it in a more traditional way by standing back and letting my zoom lens get the shot. But then viewers would not have seen the faces of the two young adults as they went from empty, blank expressions to awareness, anger, and anxiety. No one would have seen the looks on the faces of firefighters, doing their best to save lives and being frustrated by the ungrateful reactions of the two who nearly died. Viewers were able to see that these drug users weren't like many that they might see on the streets. These were two well-groomed young adults, with a young child, in an expensive truck, parked in the middle of downtown, passed out and minutes away from death.

I recognized that the elements were all there to tell a compelling story that could truly make a difference, so I jumped all in. If that's media sensationalism, maybe we need more of it.

16: Reporting during COVID

Reporting from a COVID vaccination site soon after the vaccine became available.

I HAD A FUNNY FEELING THIS WAS GOING to be big. During early 2020, I noticed there were lots of videos from news outlets in Asia that showed people wearing masks. These weren't just researchers working in labs, but people going about their daily business, walking on city sidewalks, driving, even attending events. The first cases of COVID-19 were being reported in the West, but not with too much anxiety. Maybe it was based on experience or just a gut feeling, but I thought that this new virus had the potential to be really bad. I mentioned to my daughter-in-law that ordering those masks now might be a good idea. Even so, I never imagined it would be as bad as it became in just a few short weeks.

When the first cases were reported in the United States, we still didn't realize the magnitude of what was to come. But once the number of cases and deaths rose exponentially, we began to take it seriously. In our newsroom, there was the realization that this might be a major news story. We didn't know for how long.

It was during the second or third week in March that the Carolinas and the rest of the US began to shut down. Church services were abruptly canceled, schools closed, restaurants and businesses locked their doors. My station reported a story on March 18, 2020, that the company that owned three large local shopping malls would be closed until March 29. A worker at a store in popular SouthPark Mall applauded the decision, but added a note of uncertainty, saying, "My company, thank God, is going to be taking care of the staff for at least the two weeks, but if it extends longer than that, then we're not sure what's going to happen."

As a news reporter, of course, I had to be right out in the middle of it, and this is where the job of a local reporter is truly one of public service. I could not stay home. You have information that can save lives, and you have to present it in a responsible way. One of the first stories I did about the pandemic was on March 13 about NASCAR postponing races at Atlanta Motor Speedway and Miami-Homestead due to the spread of COVID. Since the Charlotte area is home to the majority of race teams, the news was significant, even though it was not clear yet what the impact would be at Charlotte Motor Speedway. At that time, the track had issued a statement saying it was "closely monitoring facts and in frequent communication with public health officials" in regard to the major car show and swap meet known as AutoFair scheduled for April 2–5.

With things suddenly changing all around us, I documented this new "life during the pandemic."

On March 22, my wife and I drove around Salisbury to find some of the images that told the story of the new reality. That Saturday was a glorious spring day, with a few clouds in the sky, azaleas and dogwoods in beautiful bloom. But the streets of Salisbury were nearly empty. No one was on the sidewalks. In a Food Lion grocery store, there were many empty shelves, particularly where the bath tissue and diapers were kept. On the bread aisle was a sign that limited customers to two loaves. The Cinemark movie theater, usually busy on Saturday, was closed. Churches that were in the Lenten season in the build-up to Easter were closed that weekend, and most would not reopen for more than a year. At Stallings Memorial Baptist Church, members were encouraged to drive by the back of the church to pick up palm branches to celebrate Palm Sunday. A sign on the bench encouraged families to take one branch for each child to wave and suggested posting a picture on social media.

The marquee at the Meroney Theater in downtown Salisbury where a popular local theater company stages its productions, simply said, "See You Soon." Walmart was open, but had an elaborate maze of yellow tape set up in the parking lot that led people to the entrance in an attempt to keep people socially distanced. A popular Italian restaurant had signs up in the parking lot urging customers to call in an order or make an order online, adding that they would bring the food out to customers' cars. A playground at one church resembled a crime scene with yellow tape that police use to mark an unsafe area. A sign on the yellow tape had a message in all caps: "PLAYGROUND CLOSED—NO PLAY."

Other restaurants were either closed or displayed signs saying, "Takeout Only." College BBQ, a popular and long-established restaurant in business for more than fifty-five years in Salisbury, moved the booths from inside to the parking lot outside. That worked for a few days, before the state informed them that it was not an option. The tables went back inside, and the owner pushed the drive-thru options and hoped that customers would continue to support the business.

"Scared to death," said James Owen, the restaurant's owner, when I asked him about it. "That sums it up. Scared to death." I interviewed him for several stories over the years of the pandemic to track the progress of the restaurant. James was fortunate. Through takeout orders and a lot of community support, he was able to keep the restaurant open, and happily, it is thriving again today. The restaurant isn't the same as it was prior to the pandemic, though. Partitions were built between booths and some tables were taken out to give diners more space.

In an interview for a story on WBTV in 2021, James expressed his gratitude for the community support. "The only way I can sum it up is that I was blessed, very blessed," James said. "I was fortunate enough that I had a facility that could adapt with the times, the changing times. And the times have changed. It's the most humbling thing I've ever been through in my life. The support from the community was absolutely tremendous, and you know, you never know where your help is going to come from. The number of people who showed up like they were my best friend—I've never seen before. It was amazing, amazing."

Another popular restaurant wasn't as fortunate. Wink's BBQ tried the takeout-only option when the pandemic began in March 2020, but closed its doors just four months later.

"This doesn't mean God let us down," said second-generation owner Byron Martin. Martin was not just a business owner, but he's a personal friend that I have known for years. Reporting on that restaurant closing was difficult for me. "It's going to be okay. We'll get through it, it's just another problem, it's nothing, nothing that's going to stop things, so that was difficult to get to that point, to come to that . . . wow," Martin told me in an interview. "It wasn't sustainable. We had our busy times, and that was it."

In March, I also reported on local efforts to set up relief funds through the local United Way, drive-thru COVID testing at the Veterans Administration Medical Center in Salisbury, and the suspension of visitation at state prisons across North Carolina. The first deaths in our viewing area were reported on March 25, 2020. A person in their late seventies from Cabarrus County died from complications associated with the virus, according to state health officials. The patient had several underlying medical conditions. A second person, in their sixties from Virginia, who was traveling through North Carolina, also died from COVID-19 complications.

There were positive stories during the pandemic. In August 2020, I reported on the story of ninety-seven-year-old Rosa Lee Tyson, who had spent three weeks in the hospital with COVID, but recovered and was able to come home. I sat with her and her son in the small kitchen of their home in Salisbury. Tyson looked well, smiling and gesturing with her hands as she spoke with me. "I feel good," she told me. Her son, Daniel Haddock, added, "I couldn't even hardly tell my fiancée how happy I was . . . she had beat the virus, and she was coming here. She took care of us for all of our lives, right, and now it's time for us to take care of her," Haddock said.

Rosa "Granny" Lee Tyson lived for another sixteen months before dying at the age of ninety-eight. The story that I did with her proved to be popular and was picked up by TV stations across the country. It did offer some hope at a time when hope seemed to be in short supply.

Unfortunately, for every story like Ms. Tyson's, there were many more where the outcome was tragic. One of the largest nursing homes in the area that I covered for WBTV was The Citadel in Salisbury. It would gain notoriety as the home of the largest and deadliest COVID cluster outbreak in North Carolina. By the time it finally closed, there had been 168 confirmed cases and twenty-one deaths reported at this facility.

Located on Julian Road near Interstate 85, The Citadel was partially hidden by large trees that filled its front yard. When I reported stories there, we used our helicopter to get a full view of the complex that many people had never seen. One of the first stories I reported was published online in April 2020. By then, The Citadel already had more than 100 people diagnosed with COVID, according to the state.

That month, a personal injury lawsuit was filed in Rowan County court on behalf of the family of a resident at the facility. Lawyers representing an elderly woman who was seriously ill with COVID-19 claimed negligence and reckless conduct on the part of Citadel management and staff, and demanded a jury trial. The suit alleged that The Citadel was "poorly staffed," and that during an inspection in February 2020, it had received a report that reflected "unsafe and unsanitary" conditions. Corrective action was not taken, according to the suit, resulting in the creation of a "lethal and growing reservoir of the severe acute respiratory syndrome coronavirus 2," which is the "causative agent of the COVID-19 disease."

"Just imagine if it was your mother or your father or one of your relatives in that situation; you want them to get the best care possible. I find it pretty bad," said a family member of one of the residents.

"He tells me that certain ones [caregivers] are just very mean, you know . . . to him," said Pat Cohen, who had a brother at The Citadel. "I'm thinking that they don't have enough help there so the people are displacing their anger; they're putting it on the residents."

Wallace & Graham, a local law firm, represented several of the residents of The Citadel and their families as more and more cases came to light. In one affidavit, a resident's family member said she only became aware of the outbreak through news reports and couldn't find out if her mother had been tested. The woman removed her mother from The Citadel and said that three days later, her mother tested positive for COVID-19. Another woman said there was a lack of communication and that she and her family had a hard time getting information about her mother. She said staff gave conflicting updates on her mother's condition and that on April 15, 2020, as she was preparing to do a video call with her mom, the doctor suddenly told her that her mother was dead from COVID-19.

State officials stepped in, law enforcement was involved, and I reported on every development. Officials from The Citadel and its parent company refused to speak with me or any other reporters. They did manage to go on social media and complain about my reporting and how they were portrayed in the media. Other staff members privately messaged me to say they appreciated what we were bringing to light, then adding that things were even worse than I had been reporting. I spent hours over two years interviewing family members off-site and standing on the right-of-way in front of the facility to do my live shots and tell the stories.

One day, I was standing in my usual spot on the industrial property next to The Citadel. That was a place that was right next to Citadel property, from which we were banned, and it still gave us a good view of the building to have in the background of the live shots, and a way to see the comings and goings in the parking lot. On this particular day I was treated with something much better than the usual sight of hearses going up the driveway or workers making obscene gestures. A member of the management spotted me and walked toward me. Earlier that day, a "strike team" from the Centers for Disease Control had paid a surprise visit to the facility as the number of COVID cases and deaths mounted. I wasn't sure what to expect, so I made sure my camera was on and rolling. To my surprise, the woman was willing to answer a few questions. The official turned out to be the Chief Operating Officer of Accordius Health, the company that owned The Citadel. She began by telling me that the CDC visit was "a win."

"No smoking gun, no smoking gun; I think they found everything to be in place," the Accordius Health COO told me during a brief on-camera interview. "I think that part of what they took away from here was that because there was a large outbreak here several months ago, they came in expecting to see something much worse than it actually was, I think," the COO said. "When you hear about the center you think, oh my gosh, it really must be alarming to walk inside. It's not. It's peaceful, it's calm, staff are working."

But over the next two years, things did not improve. There were more deaths, more lawsuits, then finally in early 2022, the federal Centers for Medicare and Medicaid Services sent a letter to The Citadel informing management that Medicare would no longer pay The Citadel for services. That loss of funding usually means the end for nursing facilities.

The letter announcing the termination was a stinging rebuke to the management, who continued to insist that improvements had been made. In part, the letter from the government said:

The Citadel Salisbury has continued to be out of substantial compliance after multiple on-site health and safety surveys (February 19, 2021; September 2, 2021; and March 4, 2022) documented a failure to comply with several federal requirements.

Despite multiple opportunities to address its non-compliance, The Citadel Salisbury did not demonstrate that it can ensure the health, safety, and well-being of its residents. The facility has had a cyclic pattern of immediate jeopardy, substandard quality of care and actual harm to residents.

On June 14, 2022, The Citadel closed its doors. On June 23, 2022, standing on the familiar spot right next door, I did my last story on The Citadel, noting the various problems that had been found over the prior two years, from the COVID outbreak to unsanitary conditions, low staffing, and other infractions that led to the closure.

The COVID pandemic was a time that I was able to do some of the most impactful reporting of my career, and much of it was never seen on TV. In early 2020, after the pandemic began, I started recording daily updates that I posted on the WBTV-Salisbury Facebook page. Nearly every weekday morning, I would set up my camera prior to six a.m., then record myself giving an update on the pandemic and highlighting positive things that were happening in the community. Each video was between six and eight minutes long.

A typical video began with me saying hello, and then sharing a couple of really awful dad jokes for levity. I then gave the update on numbers from the Rowan County Health Department. They posted an update each day that included the number of new cases, number of deaths, number of people hospitalized due to COVID, number of people who had recovered, and number of active cases in the county. There were days that those numbers were alarming, with a half dozen or more deaths and many new cases. I then highlighted some of the positive things happening, such as drive-by birthday parties, parades to show support for medical workers, and ways people were coping with the isolation of lockdowns. I also made sure to include any updates from the health department or from city and county officials on things residents needed to know. At the end of each video, I tried to offer something hopeful, then closed it out with, "We're going to get through this, and we'll get through it together." These videos had a greater impact than I ever imagined. On a typical day, they would be viewed between 30,000 and 50,000 times, but there were days when the number of times the individual video was shared would cause the number of views to exceed 100,000. The highest viewership I recall was more than 500,000, and this was coming from a Facebook page that had a total following of 40,000. I couldn't fully understand why the videos were so popular, other than the viewers knew that I was sincere, and it provided a distraction that stepped away, briefly, from the ongoing bad news that was being shared.

When I began working as a reporter, my goal was to approach the job like it was a public service position. I recognized that between the television audience, later combined with the website and then with social media, I had a tremendous platform that WBTV allowed me to use to provide information that was truly important. I wasn't a hero like those first responders, but I could tell the stories of heroes, working to keep people safe during a very unusual time in world history. It was, I felt, my responsibility, and one of the reasons God allowed me to have this job. People were depending on me to provide what they needed and to get it right.

The pandemic videos were important, but involved a lot of work. It was something I was doing on my own time. Once I shot my part of the video, I had to edit each one by adding in video from local events, pictures, and sometimes soundbites from interviews I had done. I always wanted to make sure the video was posted to the page by 7:15 a.m., so that it would be up for the parts of the day where viewership would peak.

I usually read the comments each day. Most of them were positive, thanking me for providing the information, responding to how bad my jokes were and offering their own, and telling me about other positive events that I could include in future videos. But after about a year or so, I noticed an unwelcome change in the comments and in some of the private messages that I was sent. Many people had had enough of the restrictions, the masks, the social distancing, and the shutdowns. People began to blame the media, and since I was a loud local voice on the issue, I took a lot of criticism. Some folks accused me of being an agent of the conspiracy and said that the numbers I gave from the health department were all false. That kind of criticism genuinely hurt. My only motivation had been to help my community, and now some were accusing me of lying to them. The video that I produced while getting my COVID vaccine in the parking lot of a former shopping mall was a particular target for scorn by those who were opposed to the vaccine. According to them, that jab showed them I was clearly working for Satan.

Even though the negative comments were a very small part of the overall feedback, they got to be enough for me to stop doing the videos. I still gave the updates as part of my usual news reporting, but the personal touch was gone. For weeks, I received messages from people asking me to bring back the videos, but I just didn't want to see the rubbish comments anymore. Looking back on it now, I'm glad that I did that extra bit of work and I believe it did help my community. To this day, I run into people who will stop me and tell me how much the videos meant to them.

I did meet some extraordinary people during the pandemic, even if it took heart-wrenching circumstances to bring us together. Shane Dwight Peoples manages a popular comic-book shop in Salisbury. He's a great guy with a sense of humor that will keep you in stitches. He's also a person who was deeply wounded by the loss of both of his parents due to COVID.

You may have seen the story of Johnny Lee and Cathy Darlene Peoples. It was reported locally, but also nationally and internationally. The hook for the story was that in September 2020, they died in the hospital, holding hands, within minutes of each other.

"They were married forty-eight years, been together fifty years. They walked hand in hand for those fifty years," Shane told me in our first interview. It marked the end of a thirty-day ordeal of both parents contracting the virus, rapidly declining, and then dying. It started with his mother, just days away from retirement.

"It was mainly the fever and loss of taste," Peoples said at the time. "My dad started showing symptoms two days later. About two weeks later, they were both put in the ICU. Everything just went south, everything just got worse." And when the end was in sight, Shane says the hospital staff did what they could to bring the couple together.

"The next day they put them in the same room, same ICU room, they put their hands together, the nurses gathered around, and they passed within four minutes of each other," Peoples said.

In a widely read post on Facebook, Shane poured out his heart, remembering his parents, but also encouraging people to take COVID seriously so that they wouldn't have a similar experience:

"I miss them so very much. I'm not sure how I'm going to deal without being able to talk to them every night on my ride home from work or not being able to send them pictures and videos of my family. I'll never be able to hug them again. I'll never hear Mom sing happy birthday to anyone, again. I'll never see them smile when they see Liam and Ava come into the room. They won't get to see their grandchildren grow up, or see many of their grandchildren graduate.

I know a lot of people believe they have/had the most loving, most caring, affectionate, and devoted parents, but they are wrong. That's my parents. I only wish I could fill their shoes.

Hold your family close. Treat every moment with them like it's your last, it could very well be. Love and keep on loving.

I just wish everyone could see them through my eyes. You would see the two most loving and caring couple, ever. Without them, this world just got a bit more gloomy.

Sorry this was so long.

Love all of you.

Wear a mask.

Wash your hands.

Practice social distancing.

Be kind to each other."

I interviewed Shane several more times through the pandemic and did a story on the day that he and his wife got in line in the mall parking lot to get the vaccine. They sat together on a cold morning in March 2021, in Shane's red Nissan Rogue, and waited their turn to pull under the large temporary awning to get the second dose of the vaccine.

"It's wonderful," Peoples told me. "On the way up here, I just thought about calling my mom and telling her that we're getting the second dose and it hit hard. I wish my parents were here to get their vaccines."

Shane's story inspired many, and also angered some who remained opposed to the vaccine. Shane told me he even got push-back at the comic-book store from customers who did not wish to wear the mask inside the store. When Shane told the customers the very personal reason he preferred for them to be masked up, he said that most apologized and complied with the request, but others just walked out.

I still visit Shane at the comic-book store. I enjoy being able to talk with him now, off the record, not as a reporter, but as a friend. When I look back on my days of covering the pandemic, his is the first face that comes to mind. I'm grateful to know him; I just wish we could have become friends under happier circumstances.

From a technical standpoint, covering the pandemic as a news story changed the way I did my job. The biggest change was in the process of crafting a story. Normally, that would involve doing interviews on camera with the subjects of the story, as well as with some kind of an official relevant to that story. The pandemic forced us to come up with new ways to share stories.

Zoom became the go-to outlet for doing interviews. With this tool, reporters could just look at their phones while the subject on the other end of the call did the same thing. The call was recorded directly from the phone, so the video and audio quality was usually pretty good. The early days of Zoom did present a learning curve for us all, though. Many of the people interviewed on Zoom put the phone flat down on the desk, which presented an unflattering "up the nose" shot with the ceiling in the background.

I hated doing Zoom interviews and would try anything I could to get out of doing them. I would ask if they were comfortable with me doing the interview in person, but socially distanced. Most agreed. My method involved showing up at the location early and letting the person know I was outside. I would take a microphone and put it on a mic stand and set up my camera anywhere from fifteen to twenty feet away, then let the interviewee know I was ready. The subject would come out and stand at the mic while I asked my questions. I liked this set-up better, because it showed that I was going to the effort to genuinely get in front of that person to ask the questions that needed asking. It also looked and sounded better.

I did use Zoom for interviews with people who lived outside of our coverage area, or when some people were just adamant about no personal contact, but I tried to get by without it as much as I could. Toward the end of the pandemic, many people I interviewed figured out how to make their Zoom shot look better. They had small tripods for the phones with a ring light to make their faces look better. They also figured out how to place in the background some items that told viewers more about who they were. You'd see awards, books, posters—anything that showed some personality, and was certainly an improvement over the nose/ceiling shots.

Reporters took on a new look during those days, too. WBTV ordered everyone on air in the field to wear a COVID mask. I understood the reasoning behind it; we couldn't very well keep telling people about mask mandates if we were standing there with our bare-naked faces exposed. The first COVID mask I had was given to me by an officer with the Salisbury Police Department. It was dark blue and had been part of a large bag of masks given to the police by a citizen. The first time that I wore it on air was followed by several messages from followers on social media telling me how ridiculous it was. In a way, they were correct. Since I worked by myself, I was usually alone when I did a live shot during the afternoon news shows. It was just me standing in front of a camera on a tripod, and usually there was no one anywhere around me. The station's take on it was that viewers couldn't know if I was alone or not, and that it would be inconsistent for me not to wear the mask when every other reporter was masked up. There were a couple of times that I was reporting live from the Blue Ridge Parkway, with nothing around me for miles except bears and squirrels, but I was still wearing a mask.

A few months into the pandemic, I saw a gaiter in a local fishing tackle shop. It's like a mask, only it goes below your chin and covers your neck and you could pull it up over your mouth and nose. I bought one and tried it out on air the next week. I liked it because it was something you could wear all the time and just pull it up when you needed to. I thought it was more convenient, comfortable, and it looked cool too. I had worn it for about a week when the station started getting complaints. Viewers were citing studies that said the gaiter was not thick enough to serve as an effective COVID mask, and that it was dangerous for me to be on air, seemingly giving my approval to this method. Off it came. I faithfully wore a proper mask until that mandate was finally lifted.

Thankfully, I never got sick during the actual pandemic. I did get COVID in 2023, but it was a very mild case, not much worse than a cold. However, I knew several people personally who died from COVID when the pandemic was at its worst, and many of my coworkers came down with the virus while we were trying our level best to stay on message and provide the information that would help the public.

I've always felt that it was my responsibility as a journalist to serve my community, and the COVID pandemic was a time where that was more important than ever. I shared everything I could that local and state officials offered about staying safe, but I also used my humor, personality, and local roots to assure viewers and readers that I was in the middle of this just like they were, and that we would get through it together.

18: Kannapolis Rising

Built near the site of the former Cannon Mills textile plant, the City Hall stands as a symbol of a community reborn with a new purpose.

COVERING LOCAL NEWS IN THE SAME COMMUNITY for more than thirty years gave me the opportunity to see the rise and fall of many businesses, people, institutions, and even cities and towns. The ebb and flow of crime trends, economics, and the movement of people changed the face of my coverage area, and I was on the front row to witness these changes. As many as there have been, I don't think any place has changed as drastically as the city of Kannapolis.

Kannapolis is located between Salisbury and Concord, about thirty minutes north of Charlotte on Interstate 85. The population as of 2022 was right around 58,000 and growing. For many years, it was what everyone called a mill town. The huge Cannon Mills textile plant was the largest employer for decades. Cannon Mills was founded in 1887 by James Cannon. The name of the city reflected its identity. Kannapolis means "city of looms." Every day, thousands of mill workers clocked in and out at what was the largest textile plant in the United States, making bed pillows, down comforters, mattress pads, blankets, and throws.

When I was growing up in Salisbury, I didn't hear much about Kannapolis and rarely went there. The larger city of Concord had a big shopping mall and lots of restaurants, so we usually just drove past "Ktown" and went a little farther south on I-85 for a night out.

When I started working at WBTV, Kannapolis was already changing. The textile industry in the US was taking a hit from cheaper imports, and textile plants in other countries could produce goods with a much lower labor cost. Cannon Mills had gone through ownership changes, from the Cannon family to billionaire David Murdock, to Fieldcrest Mills, and then to Pillowtex. More than 4,800 workers in Cabarrus and Rowan County plants kept clocking in every day and hoping for the best.

One of the most significant days of my career was July 30, 2003. I began that day in Kannapolis at the hall rented by the UNITE union. There had been rumors for weeks about potential layoffs at Pillowtex, and the UNITE hall was a good place for me to go to find workers who were usually willing to speak with me as I covered the story. When I arrived on the morning of July 30, I knew something was going on because of the hushed conversations and the looks on the faces of the workers who had stopped by. One of them told me he had just heard that the plant was closing today. *Closing*? I wouldn't have been surprised by some layoffs, but I didn't really think there was a danger that this iconic plant that employed thousands of people could abruptly shut down. It was not confirmed, but I knew I had to get over to the plant to see what I could find out.

When I pulled up to the main gate, I noticed several Kannapolis police cars and private security officers. The blue-and-white police cars with lights flashing were parked near the main entrance to the plant. People were coming out of the large administrative office building carrying boxes with their belongings, like desk lamps, pillows, and house plants. People were crying and hugging one another. While what I witnessed seemed to confirm the rumors, that wasn't enough for me to report that the plant had actually closed. I made calls to Pillowtex executives, the public relations team, the union, the NC Department of Commerce, local and state politicians, and city officials. I can't remember exactly which official gave me the confirmation that I needed, but someone did, and we broke the story on the noon news that Pillowtex had shut down. That meant more than 7,600 workers company-wide and nearly 4,800 in North Carolina were suddenly unemployed.

I stayed outside the front entrance to the plant all day, doing several live shots for WBTV and for other stations that wanted to report this news. In the early afternoon, a group of fifteen to twenty people were forming a circle in the park directly across the street. They joined hands and began praying for the displaced workers and their families and for decisions that would be made over the coming weeks. They acknowledged the disappointment of the mill closure, but held out hope that something good would eventually come from it. I shot video of them praying, and then I joined in with them.

A reflection published by the City of Kannapolis in 2023 includes this observation from Darrell Hinnant, who had been recently elected to the city council when the shutdown came: "People were in shock. They had tears dripping off of their chins. Some were collapsing on the sidewalk. They had no clue what they were going to do."

The sudden closure turned out to be the largest one-day job loss in North Carolina's history. Workers I interviewed on that day all said they had heard the rumors of a shutdown, a bankruptcy, another sale, but they never thought the plant would shut down. Many of them lived in mill houses and were second- or third-generation mill workers. They had never known life without the mill and had no idea what they would do now.

Among the quotes I heard that day from workers:

"I could go back to school; my husband could get a full-time job instead of unemployment."

"You sit here waiting, wondering what tomorrow is going to be."

"Number one, if you've got another job, take it. If you don't, get your skill level up."

"I'm downhearted; it's devastating."

David Coone, a worker at Pillowtex for thirty-seven years, told me: "Well, I had heard rumors, you know, and I was on when they called me, told me the job had been terminated."

I reported on the closure for the next few weeks, every single day. The impact stretched well beyond Kannapolis. Many other businesses were suppliers to Pillowtex, and many of them were closing too as a result of the Pillowtex shutdown. Local officials came together with elected leaders from the state and from the federal government. A Rapid Response Team was set up to work through Rowan-Cabarrus Community College to help retrain workers and find jobs in other areas. Churches close to the plant began organizing food drives and looking for other ways to help displaced workers. On one of these days, the plant reopened to allow the mill workers to go back inside and retrieve their belongings from the floor. Men pushed huge tool chests, nearly as big as those "war wagons" that NASCAR teams have in their pit stalls, across Main Street to their pickup trucks. Many of the tool boxes were covered with stickers of their favorite race teams or vacation spots, or any other entity to show their individual personalities. The boxes were a bit beaten up, but they were the very tools of the trade that allowed these workers to do their jobs for decades. As they were pushing the carts along, I asked many of them how long they had worked at the plant. Many replied, citing thirty, forty, even fifty years. It seemed like these former workers, just like the tools they were pushing, had been built for their specific job, and like those tools, would be resistant and unsuitable to ever do anything else.

In 2004, the University of North Carolina at Chapel Hill published a twenty-nine-page paper called the "Community Response to the Pillowtex Textile Kannapolis Closing: The Rapid Response Team as a Facilitative Device." It included demographic information on the displaced workers that showed that 70 percent of them were unwilling to consider relocation from Cabarrus and Rowan counties, 93 percent could not afford health insurance, and that by the first week of August, only a week after the closing, 43 percent reported being behind in rent or mortgage payments with over 10 percent receiving eviction or foreclosure notices.

This study showed that the average age of a displaced worker was forty-six. Sixty percent were men, 40 percent were women, and about half had a high school education. I went door-to-door in the mill houses near the plant to interview these people. Many told me they were intimidated by the thought of going back to school and trying to learn a new skill. Very few had any computer skills, but they knew that such knowledge would likely be very important for their futures.

At this point, a lot of people were writing the obituary for the City of Kannapolis. Foreclosures and repossessions were up following the plant closure and local businesses were closing. The city took a substantial hit to its tax base. How could it recover? What could be done? How could such a purpose-built town reinvent itself? How could thousands of workers who only knew one skill ever adapt to a new economy?

It turned out that the city of looms was just beginning to weave a brand-new story.

I stayed with this story for the rest of my career. I reported about workers being retrained at the community college to learn to be truck drivers, HVAC workers, or in other fields. That was good, but it was a piecemeal recovery that, in the long run, couldn't bring the city back to where it needed to be. Something unexpected was needed, and that's exactly what came to pass.

Less than five years after the closure, former owner David Murdock was back in Kannapolis, this time to announce the development of the 350-acre campus that would be home to a public-private partnership called the North Carolina Research Campus (NCRC). It was built on the very spot where the now demolished textile mill once stood. According to Murdock, the NCRC was created to "foster collaboration and further knowledge in biotechnology, nutrition, agriculture, and health."

I covered the dedication ceremony held in October 2008. It included then US Senator and Salisbury native Elizabeth Dole, US

18: Kannapolis Rising

Senator Richard Burr, US Congressman Robin Hayes, and Lieutenant Governor Beverly Perdue, along with former Governors James Hunt and James Martin. Dozens more state and local politicians and business and education leaders also attended.

"The possible collaboration of the different entities at the NC Research Campus is endless and will be the start of a whole new era of collaborative research and innovation to benefit mankind," Murdock said during the dedication. "And that's good news for a world needing to hear good news."

There was also the good news about jobs that Murdock thought would be created by the NCRC. The estimate was that the campus would create 30,000 new jobs within twelve years. Unemployment was still high in the area in early 2008, so this projection sounded good, until the realization set in that many of these jobs would require a college education and, in many cases, advanced degrees.

The early burst of enthusiasm around the NCRC cooled with the reality of the recession in 2008. The original plans that called for several new buildings and a specialized school that would serve the state were significantly changed. The campus was built, anchored by the imposing David Murdock Core Lab, with additional buildings in a horseshoe-shaped pattern around a large green space. Appalachian State University, Duke University, North Carolina A&T State University, North Carolina Central University, North Carolina State University, University of North Carolina at Chapel, University of North Carolina at Charlotte, University of North Carolina at Greensboro, and Rowan-Cabarrus Community College are among the institutions that have a presence on the campus.

Groundbreaking research is now being done in Kannapolis.

Much of what is being studied has to do with how diet affects the human lifespan. In 2022, for example, I reported on a story that focused on the health benefits of elderberry syrup and how it can be effective against colds and flu and how it can affect brain health when it comes to memory loss and dementia. In 2022, I reported that Duke Kannapolis had fifty-eight funded research projects with 110 Duke faculty, as well as dozens of collaborations with investigators and institutions outside of Duke. Their areas of work include COVID-19, pain, mental health, smoking cessation, type 2 diabetes, cardiovascular disease, aging, chronic kidney disease, and more.

As great and prestigious as the NCRC is, it didn't do everything officials were hoping for in terms of job creation and tax base. That was going to take something more.

In 2015, the Kannapolis City Council negotiated an agreement to buy forty-six acres of downtown property from David Murdock. The city agreed to pay $5.5 million for just over 653,000 square feet of buildings that included a historic movie theater, the city offices, a bank building, and the former site of one of the Cannon Mills plants. The purchase included a shopping area known as Cannon Village that now consisted mainly of empty storefronts.

"This purchase of property will allow us to better plan and stimulate development in our downtown core. In order to best capitalize on this opportunity, we will develop a long-range strategic plan," Kannapolis City Manager Mike Legg said at the time.

Mike Legg was always one of my favorite officials to interview. He is friendly and forthright and surprisingly accessible for a public figure. Just about anytime I needed him for an interview, he would make himself available. He spent a lot of time with me in front of city hall, patiently waiting for me to set up the camera, put the mic on his lapel, then ask questions for an interview that would usually be cut down to a trim twenty or thirty seconds for use in a story that would last a minute and a half or two minutes on TV. Of course, for the most part the stories were very positive as I tracked the growth of the city.

"We simply cannot afford to not invest in our downtown. The expected direct return on our investment means millions of dollars in jobs, services, and products, which will be available to our citizens. People want to live, work, and play in the downtown," said Kannapolis Mayor Darrell Hinnant.

Why take the gamble? City leaders were betting that the area was ripe for new commercial development, and they believed that if they owned it all, they could better do what potential buyers would need when it came to infrastructure and other details. The Kannapolis "moon shot" paid off quickly. Within a year, there were developers announcing plans for downtown. I reported in August 2016 that a developer had been signed for the first project, and as it turned out, it was truly the tip of the iceberg.

Over the next few years, Kannapolis city leaders announced project after project. The minor league baseball team based in Kannapolis that played its games in a stadium near I-85 was sold to a new owner in 2018, and a new stadium was built right in the heart of downtown, right where part of the old Cannon Mills plant once stood. The newly named Kannapolis Cannon Ballers, a minor league affiliate of the Chicago White Sox, loved the new ballpark, and it served as the anchor for the development of the old Cannon Village.

In July 2022, I reported that city leaders were saying that all the downtown properties purchased in 2015 were now spoken for. "By the end of this year, every parcel here in downtown will be committed, sold, on the way to either be permitted or under construction," Mayor Hinnant told me.

I recently learned from the city's Public Information Officer Annette Privette Keller that the downtown property tax values have gone from $18 million to $118 million since the downtown properties were purchased.

The vision of 2015 had come to fruition beyond people's wildest expectations. The area that was Cannon Mills and the Cannon Village is now a revitalized downtown space. There are very wide sidewalks in front of blocks of new retail stores, restaurants, and services. There are two large apartment buildings and streets of new townhomes. The city holds its annual Christmas parade at night, and with everything covered in Christmas lights, it's truly a spectacle. The downtown revitalization and streetscape has been so successful that neighboring cities are doing their own makeovers in a similar style.

Covering the rebirth of this city has been one of the most rewarding aspects of my career. I got to see the city in its lowest moment and then witness a transformation many never would have believed possible. I got to carry my camera and microphone around when that massive plant was still up and running and workers were still filing in and out on shift change carrying metal lunch boxes. I got a front-row seat for the demolition of the plant, including the moment when the two huge red brick smokestacks and an iconic red-and-white checkered water tower came crashing to the ground. I was there for the groundbreaking for the NCRC, and then for several more dirt-turning events over the years for the downtown streetscape, the new ballpark, the apartment buildings, and several other projects. Most recently, the city has added industrial parks near I-85 that have snagged companies such as Amazon, Chick-fil-A, and Gordon Food Service.

Covering Kannapolis, especially over the last few years when nearly every story was positive, was also a way for me to reset from those days when I had to cover the stories that mentally took me to a place that I didn't want to go, and for one of those stories, the dam was finally about to break.

19: Erica Parsons III

photo credit: Rowan Sheriff's Office

IN 2014, A YEAR AFTER ERICA PARSONS had been reported missing, Casey and Sandy Parsons pleaded not guilty to seventy-six counts of fraud and identity theft. Prosecutors said the couple continued to accept federal adoption assistance money for years after Erica Parsons was no longer in their home and likely no longer alive. After entering the plea, both paid an unsecured bond of $25,000 and left federal custody to await trial. But leaving the courthouse while being chased by a horde of media wasn't as easy as they likely hoped.

I was there, along with WBTV photographer Corey Schmidt. We were both holding a camera and mic, waiting to see if Casey and Sandy would make any comment. Crews from at least five other TV stations were right there with us. As Casey came out, she pushed aside the microphones and glared at the cameras as I and other reporters shouted our questions.

"Where is Erica?"

"What did you do with the money?"

"Is Erica dead?"

Another Parsons family member had brought their car as near to the door as he could get it. Casey and Sandy hurried to jump inside, along with their older biological daughter. The driver was in too much of a hurry, though, hitting the gas before the daughter could get in, dumping her on the pavement as he tried to pull away. The woman wasn't hurt and quickly jumped up and ran a few steps to get in the car.

In October 2015, we learned there would be no trial for Casey Parsons. Instead, she pleaded guilty to fifteen counts, including one count of conspiracy to defraud the government, five counts of mail fraud, four counts of aiding in the preparation of a false tax return, four counts of wire fraud, and one count of aggravated identity theft.

Sandy Parsons opted to stand trial and was found guilty on all counts of federal fraud charges. He was acquitted on three elements of a single conspiracy charge, including healthcare fraud, supplemental security income fraud, and filing a false tax return.

Now, instead of telling the same story as husband and wife, Sandy Parsons was now blaming wife Casey, not only for the fraud case, but for anything that might have happened with Erica. He said during closing arguments, "That's what I got Casey for. She takes care of me." During closing arguments, the prosecutor seized on this, telling the jury that Sandy Parsons "is claiming absolute ignorance to every major event of his life."

Sentencing for the pair took place in March 2015. The two came back to federal court to learn how long they would spend in federal prison and to spend their last day together.

Sandy Parsons was sentenced to eight years in prison; three years of supervised release; $14,062 in restitution; and a special assessment of $4,300. Casey Parsons was sentenced to ten years in prison; three years supervised release; $41,814 in restitution; and a special assessment of $1,500.

Aside from the sentencing, it was during this proceeding that it became clear that the court considered Erica Parsons to have been the victim of foul play. Testimony from witnesses during the sentencing finally brought to light years of abuse and torture suffered by Erica at the hands of her adoptive parents.

Though their lawyers and some family members disagreed with its inclusion in the fraud trial, the testimony about Erica was found relevant by the judge in the case, because it showed that Erica was not living with Sandy and Casey after 2011, even though they were still accepting government checks for her upkeep.

Jamie Parsons, the adoptive brother who first reported Erica missing in 2013, testified that "nearly everyone in the family" had abused Erica routinely. He admitted that he, Casey, Sandy, and his sister had all physically abused Erica. According to Jamie's testimony, Casey would often break Erica's fingers by bending them backward. She would then make her own casts for Erica's fingers and would not take her for medical assistance.

Jamie added that Sandy would get mad and punch Erica with his fist in the back and the top of her head. Jamie said that Erica was forced to live in a closet that was often locked for hours at a time. There was no bed in the closet and she was forced to sleep on the floor, he said. She was not given access to a bathroom and when Casey found out that Erica had relieved herself in the closet, she would be beaten. Jamie also said food was often withheld from Erica, and that she was given dog food out of a can to eat.

There was also testimony about what happened on the last night Jamie saw Erica. He said she was standing in the corner being punished.

"She looked like a zombie," he testified in court. He said her face was pale-white. Jamie Parsons testified that Erica told him that she "didn't feel good, couldn't breathe too good." When Erica told Casey that she didn't feel well, Casey told Erica to "shut the fuck up" and Jamie went to bed.

Jamie said that Casey and Sandy weren't home when he woke up the next morning. When they got home later that day, his father Sandy looked sick, "like he was about to throw up," and didn't talk. Casey looked normal, he said. Jamie said when he asked Casey where Erica was, she told him they took her to her grandmother's house.

FBI Special Agent Tara Cataldo also testified during the sentencing hearing. Cataldo said that when the Parsons home was searched following the report of Erica's disappearance in 2013, that sections of a closet were removed from the house and examined. DNA from Erica Parsons's urine and/or blood were found in the carpet and on the baseboard of the section recovered.

While addressing the couple in court, Judge Thomas D. Schroeder said that he believed they had abused Erica in such an extreme manner that when something happened to her in 2011, they refused to get medical help because the abuse would be evident to any healthcare workers.

Judge Schroeder described Erica Parsons as a "defenseless little girl who only wanted to be loved," but instead was the victim of "extreme" abuse. Based on testimony heard in court, Schroeder said that he believed that Erica was forced to live in a closet in the Parsons home, that she was constantly in fear of soiling herself and being punished for it. Schroeder said he believed that Erica died in 2011 and that on the night she was punished for complaining that she felt bad, she then died and was taken and abandoned by Casey and Sandy in what the judge called a "horrible, horrible act committed in the dark of night."

"I have sentenced thousands of people over the years," Judge Schroeder told the couple, "but no case I've ever had is as disturbing as this one." Judge Schroeder called Casey Parsons "morally bankrupt," and said she had a "depraved mind." He described Sandy Parsons as having a "twisted mind."

That testimony was essential in proving the government's fraud case, but it still did not answer the question of where Erica Parsons, or her remains, were now. When asked if there had been any "viable information" on the whereabouts of Erica Parsons, FBI Agent Cataldo said no, adding that they followed several leads, but nothing was found.

Following sentencing, Casey and Sandy Parsons were immediately taken into federal custody. As it turned out, separating the two would be the crack that broke the dam that unleashed the flood of information that finally led this case to a conclusion.

In September 2016, human remains believed to be Erica Parsons were found buried in a shallow grave near a house in South Carolina that belonged to a relative of Sandy Parsons. It was Sandy Parsons who led investigators to the site. The remains were sent to the North Carolina Medical Examiner's Office for identification.

Days later, I obtained a copy of a warrant in which, for the first time, Sandy Parsons admitted physically abusing Erica. Since his conviction on fraud charges and separation from wife Casey, Sandy Parsons conducted several interviews with investigators. According to the warrant, Sandy Parsons admitted his "harsh treatment" of Erica. "The treatment included, but was not limited to, locking Erica in a closet, beating her with a belt buckle, bending her fingers back, and choking her," the warrant said.

According to that warrant, in August 2016, Sandy Parsons told Rowan County Sheriff's investigator Chad Moose that Erica was dead. Sandy Parsons said that the body was "discarded" on December 19, 2011, and that it could be found off Taylor Chapel Road in Pageland, South Carolina, near the home of his mother. Prosecutors then worked with federal authorities to release Sandy Parsons from prison so that he could take them to the burial site.

Following the discovery of Erica's remains and the warrant, I reached out again to Erica's biological mother, Carolyn. "If you ask me what I think of him now, it's not appropriate to hate people . . . I don't care. I despise every breath they're still allowed to take," she said.

Now that the remains were discovered, the investigation began moving quickly. It also finally put an end to any speculation that some were holding onto that Erica Parsons was still alive. Now, after years, the people of the community could properly mourn the little girl.

I was able to help by arranging for my church, First Baptist Church of Salisbury, to host the funeral. Dr. Kenneth Lance, the FBC pastor, readily agreed to perform the service. The church choir also agreed to sing during the service that was held in February 2017, on the day after what would have been Erica's nineteenth birthday. The funeral services were donated by a local funeral home.

"Well, we want to give closure to the community, because the community, we had always hoped for the best," said funeral director Brent Lyerly.

The sanctuary was packed with Erica's extended family members, her birth mother Carolyn Parsons, law enforcement, and members of the community who had kept up with the developments in the case. Erica's remains were placed in a small white casket in the front of the sanctuary. The casket was covered with white, pink, and purple flowers. Next to the casket was a painted portrait of Erica, based on one of the last photographs taken of her.

I, along with other members of the media, were in the large balcony overlooking the sanctuary for the funeral service. It gave us an ideal spot for our cameras to capture every moment, and we had access to the church sound board so that we could receive a direct feed of the audio without the presence of our microphones on or near the pulpit. As I looked down through the lens of my camera, I saw nearly everyone who had been part of this story over the years. Erica's mother, Carolyn, had to be helped to stay on her feet as she walked by the casket. There was Sheriff Kevin Auten, a high school classmate and lifelong friend of mine, who headed the department charged with bringing justice in the case. The investigators were there, including Chad Moose, who carried that portrait out of the sanctuary during the benediction.

As Moose carried that portrait down the aisle of the church and past the filled pews, he was also carrying something else: a burden to put behind bars the two people he knew were responsible for the torture and murder of this little girl.

"I just wanted to get her home," Moose told me. "To be honest with you, I just wanted to get the funeral done so we could move on with the case."

During his remarks, Dr. Lance said that Erica's purpose in life—and death—is to bring awareness and action against child abuse occurring "at the hands of the wicked and foolish. Erica Parsons was born into this world and given a task that she neither asked for nor deserved. She has become a symbol in this community that now cannot help but take notice."

In closing, Dr. Lance reminded the community about the responsibility of caring for children, saying that Erica had become a symbol of the struggle against child abuse.

"My faith teaches that if Erica Parsons creates within us a more attentive community, a more encouraging community, a more just community for every child, of every race, of every background, of every religion, of every point of origin, then God has redeemed her tragedy," Dr. Lance said.

And while awareness was certainly raised, there was still no accountability. Not yet. Investigators could now push harder with the case against Sandy and Casey Parsons. While they were serving their federal fraud sentences in separate prisons, detectives and the district attorney were methodically gathering what they would need to bring charges related to Erica's death. Nearly a year after the funeral, they got it.

I was working on another story in early January 2018 when I saw an email pop up in my inbox from the North Carolina State Medical Examiner. That wasn't unusual. I frequently made public records requests for autopsy results. These detailed reports show the cause of death, as well as the number and type of injuries the victim suffered and other contributing factors. Investigators usually release most of this information, and it comes out in court proceedings, but in high-profile cases it is essential information for a reporter to have. In this case, the email contained the autopsy results for Erica Parsons.

I opened the email and went straight to the line where a conclusion about cause of death was reached, and there it was: "homicidal violence of undetermined means." The coroner wrote, "we cannot exclude the possibility of a terminal blunt force injury, suffocation or strangulation." It also said that Erica suffered multiple blunt force injuries over a prolonged period of time and suffered from malnourishment and possible infections or poisonings.

The autopsy reported: "fractures documented at autopsy are consistent with multiple blunt force injuries over a prolonged period, and the growth deficit and low bone density are consistent with malnourishment. The description of the decedent just prior to her disappearance suggests she may have been suffering from untreated infection/sepsis, rhabdomyolysis, renal failure, or poisoning at that time, all of which could have caused her death."

With this conclusion reached and the information shared publicly, it seemed obvious that Sandy and Casey Parsons would be charged quickly, but that wasn't the case. When I reached out to Sheriff Auten for comment, he said that his investigators had received the email from the medical examiner at the same time that I did and that they had not had time to go over the results. On top of that, they were busy wrapping up another murder trial that had taken much of their attention for several weeks. Besides, Casey Parsons was serving her federal prison sentence in Florida while Sandy Parsons was serving his sentence in Michigan, so investigators and the district attorney had time on their side.

Six weeks later, with one unrelated murder trial completed, investigators made the announcement they had been waiting five years to make: the grand jury indicted Sandy and Casey Parsons on charges of first-degree murder, felony child abuse, felony concealment of death, and felony obstruction of justice in the death of their daughter Erica.

"It's been a long time coming. Her [Erica's] birthday would've been Saturday, she would've been twenty years old. So it's kind of fitting that we're at this point," Rowan County Sheriff Kevin Auten said. "I just wish we could've had them arrested by her birthday."

In an emotional press conference, Sheriff Auten explained that the deteriorated conditions of the remains meant that it took longer for the autopsy to be completed, but that he was relieved that his detectives and the district attorney could now move forward with the prosecution. According to the murder indictment, Casey Stone Parsons and Sandy Wade Parsons did "inflict serious bodily injury, broken and fractured bones which resulted in a permanent and protracted condition that causes extreme pain, on Erica Lynn Parsons, who was approximately twelve to thirteen years old at the time."

"There's people that think the Parsonses should have already been hung on the square," Auten said. "But they'll have their day in court. We'll let a jury decide their fate."

In the case of Casey Parsons, no jury got to hear a word about what happened to Erica. On August 2, 2019, Casey Parsons came into the superior courtroom in Rowan County to enter a guilty plea. I was in the courtroom behind my camera. The judge, who usually would not allow television cameras in her court, agreed that ongoing interest in this case, and the impact it had on the community over five years, justified the hearing being recorded and shown.

Still in federal custody, Casey Parsons was brought into the courtroom by several deputies. She was not in handcuffs or shackles and was wearing a blue-striped top and black pants. She looked like someone who had just walked in off the sidewalk. She sat at the table between her two lawyers, rarely looking around the courtroom. Her eyes were black and moved from the judge to a notepad on the desk in front of her. When given the chance to speak, she slowly and deliberately announced that she was sorry for what had happened to Erica.

"I don't know why I did the stuff I did, I'm very sorry," Casey Parsons said in court. "God gave me a precious gift, a baby girl, Erica, and he entrusted me to take care of her and I failed him and I failed Erica; I failed her horribly. My parents and my sisters reached out to me numerous times to help me. Numerous. I pushed them back. I would lie constantly to them and they would try over and over again. I was supposed to protect Erica. In the end, I failed her by choosing one child over another child. This costed her her life at the time and I want to say I'm sorry to God and to Erica, and I want to say I'm sorry to my parents and to my kids, little Sandy, Brooke, Toby, and Sadie, and my sisters, Robin and Tammy."

The one child she didn't mention by name was her son Jamie, the very person who brought Erica's disappearance to the attention of law enforcement six years earlier.

If the details about Erica's life and death that had been shared earlier in the federal fraud trials and the autopsy results weren't bad enough, there was even more disturbing testimony that came out of the plea hearing.

Birthday and Christmas gifts given to Erica were taken away and given to other kids in the family. Erica also was forced to drink from a dog bowl and sleep on a closet floor. Jamie Parsons, Erica's adoptive brother, said Casey would put Erica's hand on a hot stove, and beat her so badly that her back "looked like Jesus's back." Casey is also accused of cutting Erica's fingers open and pouring iodine on them to avoid going to the doctor.

While this information was being shared, I looked at Casey through the viewfinder of my camera. I zoomed into her face and into her eyes. I saw nothing. There were no tears, no emotion at all. She just stared straight ahead and seemed to be in a world of her own.

"What this child endured in her short life is unconscionable," said Judge Lynn Gullet as she sentenced Parsons. "This sentence will ensure that this defendant will never be around any children and it does give me great comfort to know that Erica is in a place where she will not experience any pain or sadness."

When the thirty-nine-minute hearing was over, Casey Parsons was sentenced to every day in prison that she legally could have been, which was life without the possibility of parole, plus additional consecutive sentences totaling approximately twenty-three years.

Carolyn Parsons, Erica's birth mother, was the first person I spoke with once the plea hearing ended. She thanked the investigators who played a role in the case, mentioning Rowan Sheriff's detective Lieutenant Chad Moose, Sheriff Auten, and the prosecutors. She also said she was satisfied with the plea agreement.

"Her life in prison, living, will be worse than any death sentence she could ever get," Carolyn Parsons said. "Yee-haw!" she shouted. "Casey loses her rights to watch her grandchildren grow up! What an incredible final end for her."

With Casey Parsons now going back to finish her federal prison sentence before beginning the sentence for the murder of Erica, attention turned to Sandy Parsons. A trial date had been set, but he too decided to plead guilty, and on December 17, 2019, exactly eight years since the day Erica died, Sandy Parsons was brought into court to say he was guilty.

Wearing a dark-blue suit, white shirt, and red-and-white-striped tie, closely cut hair, and glasses, forty-six-year-old Sandy Parsons walked into court looking like he could be an attorney or court official. He sat in the same chair that his wife Casey had occupied four months earlier and faced the same judge.

Judge Gullet warned those in the courtroom that the testimony would be disturbing and cautioned anyone from making any kind of outburst. Extra deputies were placed around the courtroom, just as they had been when Casey was the subject of the hearing.

Before Sandy Parsons made a statement to the court, his lawyers called a psychologist who examined Parsons several times after his arrest. She said that Parsons had been abused mentally and physically as a child by his stepfather, and that Parsons suffered from a dependent personality disorder in which he was controlled by his wife Casey. Parsons attempted suicide several times prior to his arrest, the psychologist said, and suffers now from PTSD, adding that he has nightmares and visions about burying Erica.

The attorney for Sandy Parsons wanted to show a clear difference between the role his client and Casey Parsons played when it came to Erica's murder. "Sandy Parsons's role was substantially less than that of Casey Parsons," attorney Vince Rabil said. "There is absolutely no evidence he intended for her [Erica] to die."

When it was his turn to address the court, Sandy Parsons offered an apology. "I am sorry from the bottom of my heart," Parsons said. "To my kids, to my family, to Jamie, he will always be a hero . . . to Brooklyn, Sadie, and Toby, I am sorry. To my dad and mom and step-mom, I'm sorry that I let you down. Thanks for standing behind me and helping me with my kids and grandkids. Most of all I'm sorry to Erica, as I do every night before I close my eyes. People may forgive me, I know God has, but I will never forgive myself. It makes me sick to my stomach to know what I know now what my daughter Erica went through, because a dad is there to care and to keep his children safe and to love them. I turned a blind eye as to what Erica was going through and I failed her as a dad. I also failed my other kids. I want to say thanks to Chad Moose, Rowan County detective and to Tara with the FBI. I also want to thank everybody in my community who looked for Erica and who worked on this case, and all the people in this community that prayed for her. Thanks for showing the love that she always wanted in her young life."

With that, Sandy Parsons was sentenced to serve between thirty-three and forty-three-and-a-half years in prison on the charges, which included murder, child abuse, concealment of death, and obstruction of justice. It meant that Sandy Parsons would not be getting out of prison before he was at least eighty-two years old.

Now it was over. Justice had been served. Those in the community who had followed this case closely for six years seemed satisfied with the outcome that would hold Sandy and Casey Parsons accountable for Erica's death. I felt the same way. After six years of watching those two and reporting on this case, I was satisfied with the outcome, but sick over what I had learned from the testimony. A little girl had lived a life of torture and abuse and died at the hands of the very people who were charged with living and caring for her.

This case stayed with me like few others. Between the reporting of Erica's disappearance and Sandy's plea agreement, I had to follow every step along the way for six years. Through that whole time, I continually had to ask investigators if there was anything new or anything coming up. I spent hours standing outside the courthouse and the sheriff's office with my camera and mic just waiting on Sandy and Casey to show up for some administrative matter, just so I could get new video of them and try to get them to speak with me. I made call after call to the Parsonses, to the lawyers, prosecutors, and to Carolyn Parsons and others connected to the case. I had the professional responsibility to be on top of it, but also the personal passion and curiosity that wouldn't let me ignore it. Even now, I feel nothing but hate for Casey and Sandy Parsons. I see Casey as the manipulator, while Sandy played the part of the dumb compliant stooge. To his credit, it was Sandy who eventually broke while in prison and led investigators to Erica's remains.

I always looked for the good in a story, no matter how bad it was. In this case, Erica's death brought about an awareness of child abuse and a determination by many local leaders to take steps to prevent this from happening again. The local child advocacy center known as the Terrie Hess House is the home for Prevent Child Abuse Rowan. In December 2022, the portrait of Erica that had been placed near her casket during the funeral—the same one that investigator Chad Moose lovingly carried out of the church following the service—was presented to the Terrie Hess House.

"We felt like it was time to dedicate this picture today and let it be displayed permanently in the Erica Parsons room," Sheriff Auten said. "We feel so strongly about this case and this little girl, and we're so happy we were able to get the resolution to the case that we got, and it's unfortunate that the case took place."

"I hope people see it as an example of how bad it can be and maybe some parents sometimes will put the brakes on themselves thinking about this. At least they know if they do harm a child, we're going to come together and put them away," Moose added.

As hard as this case was for the community, as difficult as it was for me to cover, it was even more of an emotional struggle for those who were closest to it: those investigators who gave Erica Parsons space in their lives and who felt the eyes of the community looking to them for justice. Lead investigator Chad Moose found a tangible way to make a connection to Erica as he worked the case.

"When I started being the primary [investigator] on this case, I saw a small purple stuffed rabbit. It was in a bag of stuffed animals in the conference room," Moose told me. He said the stuffed animals were for deputies to give to children when they are on calls where children may be frightened, or just need some kind of comforting presence. The stuffed animals are donated to the sheriff's office by local church groups. "I took the rabbit and a picture of Erica," Moose said. The picture the painting was made from. That rabbit took on special significance for Moose. Moose had made a commitment to himself that he would find Erica, and that when he did, that rabbit would be hers.

"So when we recovered her and placed her in a body bag, I placed the rabbit with her. I was worried it would probably be lost during her journey at the medical examiner. It came back when I picked her up. It was in the personal belongings bag. I placed it in the coffin with her. I didn't want her to be alone anymore," Moose added. "That rabbit was my focus and kept my rage at bay during the countless false hopes and challenges of the case."

I'm not stupid enough to think that the Erica Parsons case will somehow stop child abuse. It won't. I can only hope and pray that her example will be enough so that in at least some cases, restraint and common sense can prevail before it's too late.

20: Her Majesty, the Queen

At Westminster Abbey in London, England.

THE BIGGEST ASSIGNMENT THAT I WAS EVER given came late in my career, but it was well worth the wait. In September 2022, I was assigned to file a week of reports from London to cover the death and ultimately the funeral of Her Majesty, Queen Elizabeth II.

This was exciting to me because I'm an Anglophile and have long had a fascination with Great Britain, the royal family, and British history. That fascination started when I was a kid with Beatles music, movies like *Mary Poppins*, and the James Bond films caught my attention early, followed by Benny Hill and Monty Python. As an adult, I was captivated by the happenings of the royal family, including the Queen's anniversary and birthday celebrations and the wedding of Prince Charles and Diana.

This was the opportunity of a lifetime for a news reporter: a chance to cover world history from the front row and witness the incredible end of an era of a monarch that had ruled as head of state of the United Kingdom and fourteen other realms for more than seventy years.

But with the excitement of this assignment came a lot of apprehension. My responsibility was to find the images and people who could tell a compelling story of how folks were dealing with the loss of a revered monarch and why she meant so much to them. I planned to look for folks from the United States, and especially anyone from the Carolinas.

I had visited England before on three occasions, so I knew my way around. Each time it has been for vacation and each time was wonderful. London, Portsmouth, Leeds, and of course my hometown's counterpart of Salisbury were the places I'd enjoyed the most. I made some true friendships with several folks in London through social media and was able to meet them in person on my most recent trip five years earlier.

On the logistics side, in addition to the camera and microphone, I was loaded down like a beast of burden with a tripod, lights, big batteries, little batteries, a computer, all kinds of chargers and power supplies, and other stuff that I didn't even know how to use, but still had to lug around. And yes, I had to have the station pay extra for overweight luggage for the flight across the pond.

After I arrived, I got to work as soon as I checked into the Hilton London Paddington. Before going over to our CBS base that had been set up for the funeral, I went into the streets outside the hotel with camera and microphone and started interviewing people and capturing images of a city in mourning. The souvenir shops were already selling every item you can imagine with the Queen's picture and the date of her death.

My base was in the CBS compound on top of the Methodist Central Hall, across the street from Westminster Abbey. It was a great place to work due to its location. Thankfully, some of the CBS folks were able to help me with the technical aspects of getting my face and my stories on the air. My assignment was to report for WBTV, but also for other affiliated TV stations all over the country. I was assigned to work with Rick Folbaum, an anchor and reporter from Atlanta News First. As far as I could tell, we were the only local television reporters from the Southeast to be in London.

I couldn't miss this moment of history, so I threw everything I had into it, and therefore, my days were very long. I got by with a minimal amount of sleep during those six days and ate very little. Rick and I were up by six each morning. We met in the lobby for a delicious full English breakfast, then took one of London's famous black cabs down toward the Methodist Hall. Each day, the cabs had to let us out a little farther away from the area than the day before, due to the tight security. We had to walk for blocks carrying our equipment to the church hall. Rick and I discussed what aspect of the story we wanted to cover each day. After putting our equipment in our designated spot, we hit the streets, walking for miles to different places where we could find people to speak with and interesting images to show. They were all around us. There's an old axiom in news that "everybody has a story." In a crowd this large, there had to be thousands of stories to choose from. We walked out from the church hall and into the streets around Parliament Square, Westminster Abbey, and near the Houses of Parliament. We weren't really looking at the tourist sites, but at the faces. Experienced reporters can tell who may be up for a chat and who would rather not. We looked for Brits who were mourning their queen and American tourists, particularly any from the Carolinas or the Atlanta area. We introduced ourselves as reporters from "American television," and did enough interviews each day for both of us to put together stories.

Once I shot all the video and interviews that we needed for that day's stories, we went back to the Methodist Hall. Separately, Rick and I would write our stories. Once I got his script and his voice recording, I went to work editing. After I finished his story, I put my story together. We shared some of the interviews, but still managed to do our own unique stories. Editing video and sound on the laptop has made things much easier than in my first few years of being a reporter, but it's still time consuming, especially if you're a perfectionist like me. I had to make sure every shot added something to the story and that the stories flowed. I wanted to make sure the report included interesting information and images that folks at home might enjoy and that they wouldn't see otherwise if they were watching national networks or cable news.

We then had to do several hours of live shots for TV stations all over the country. The stations would use our recorded stories, or packages, and then we would be live at the beginning and end to give each station a custom "presence" in London. That made for very long days with no breaks.

Our broadcast position gave us a great view of Westminster Abbey, but getting in place was not for the faint of heart. The church and the network had agreed to build a temporary platform facing the Abbey, but to get out onto it we had to climb a ladder, squeeze through a window, crawl along a short and narrow plank, then climb down another ladder. Doing this while carrying equipment was a bit of a challenge. Once on the platform, we stood side-by-side with reporters and photographers from other media outlets. While the view behind me looked great, if you could have seen it from the other side, you would have been amazed that any work got done at all.

On our first day, the casket bearing the body of the late Queen Elizabeth II was led in a procession from Buckingham Palace to Westminster Hall, where her body would lie in state for five days. The procession included the thundering boom of artillery cannon salutes and ranks of soldiers both on horseback and marching in the solemn parade. There were the splendid uniforms, with Big Ben tolling in the background, and the raised coffin, or catafalque, atop a gun carriage with the imperial state crown.

Hundreds of thousands lined the streets to see the flag-draped casket. The children of Queen Elizabeth, including King Charles III, walked slowly behind. That was the first time I had seen the royal family in person.

Many along the route were crying as they stood along the road-sides in crowds many people deep, some only able to see what they had captured after blindly sticking their phones as high as their arms would allow above the throngs of mourners. There was silence along the way, broken only by the steady *clop, clop* of the horses' hooves on the streets.

If folks were in the first few rows along the sidewalks, or watching on television, they observed the sight of a family mourning the loss of a loved one and a nation mourning the loss of an icon.

I asked a London woman why it was so important to be there in person. "To say goodbye to the Queen," she said. "She's been the Queen for Great Britain and the Commonwealth, the only queen we've known, and she was so friendly and had a lovely smile."

Before the procession began, I spoke with a family from Swansea in Wales. They'd hopped in one of London's famous black cabs to find a good spot to watch the procession. When I asked them why they were there, a young girl told me, "Because I feel like I'm living in a part of history I'll never see again."

Americans, too, wanted to witness a part of history, which included the appearance of the new king, a man who had spent decades as the heir. Angela Haufschild from Wisconsin had just moved to London that week. "In light of the Queen's passing, we knew that the celebrations of her life would be going on, so we wanted to just attend because it's a pretty incredible thing to be able to be here for a moment like this. We just wanted to join in with the rest of London and pay our respects," she told me.

That night, a Wednesday, thousands stood in a line that stretched for miles around Westminster Hall so that they could walk inside for a quick glimpse of the coffin to offer their respects.

People stood for fourteen, fifteen hours in the line, and during all the waiting and shuffling forward in line, they made new friends and shared food. The appearance of British football icon David Beckham lifted spirits as he waited, along with everyone else, and shared snacks with those around him. Asked what he was eating and sharing with others in the queue, Beckham said Pringles, lemon sherbet, sandwiches, coffee, and donuts.

King Charles III and Prince William spent real time with folks in the line, thanking them for coming and accepting the condolences and well wishes of so many mourners.

My week in London was one of the hardest working weeks I

had in my career. The only break came on the Saturday before the funeral. The station said that I could have the day off and I was very appreciative and excited for the possibilities.

In the late 1960s, the Beatles spent a day going to various locations in London for a photoshoot. That day has been called their "Mad Day Out." For me, Saturday was my Mad Day Out and I wanted to make the most of it. I was up early and out the front door of the hotel by eight. I headed for the usual tourist spots and took lots of pictures along the way. I was struck by the signs of mourning in the windows of nearly every shop and office building. Some were simple handmade signs, others were large and colorful, or were stark black and white with pictures that reflected all the stages of the life of Queen Elizabeth II. Many of the businesses had video boards set up with their special message of tribute and mourning. I saw at least one office building draped in heavy black cloth.

The Hugo Boss store had a picture from the 1953 coronation. Canada House had a large and colorful recent photograph of the Queen bordered in red with the message "In Memoriam, 1926–2022." A small shop had a simple piece of copy paper with a picture of the Queen from the 1950s with the message, "Thank you, ma'am, for everything." As I walked to Trafalgar Square, near the London Eye and Tower of London and the royal parks, I stopped to take picture after picture of a nation in mourning.

As I got near Buckingham Palace, I spotted a long line of people. It wasn't a single file, in fact, it was a line that stretched for miles that was eight to ten people across. This wasn't the famous queue to see the Queen lying in state, but just a massive movement of people wanting to pass by in front of the palace to pay their respects at the monarch's former home, many leaving flowers and other tributes. I joined the line and enjoyed talking to people around me. After about ninety minutes and very slow progress, I pulled out my media badges and showed them to one of the police officers. He allowed me to jump out of line and walk to the palace. That allowed me to get there quickly and have a better view of all the people who were there.

At the palace, I spotted bouquets of flowers tied around the fence posts. Thousands of people gently placed their flowers on the ground that was already covered like a gigantic floral carpet. I started walking down the Mall that leads from Buckingham Palace to the Admiralty Arch, just taking it all in, when I heard a commotion behind me and back toward the palace. I turned to look and saw two police cars and then the large purple-and-black Bentley state limousine with the small Royal Standard on the roof. It was King Charles leaving the palace to ride out and speak to people waiting in the queue. I was thrilled! While I had seen the royal family earlier in the week during the procession, this was one of the spontaneous moments that you just live for. I grabbed my personal camera and managed to get a couple of pictures. It may sound silly, but seeing him heading out really choked me up. I called my wife at the moment and yelled, "I just saw the King!" I saw him wave from the back seat and while I'd like to say he waved at me, there were one or two other folks walking along the Mall that day who were also standing and waving.

My Mad Day Out included a stop at a barbershop. Why? I don't know. It looked like one of those fancy, upscale men's barbershops you see in those old movies with stars like Charles Laughton or Oliver Reed. The barber was Turkish, and he was a lot of fun. He told me that British Formula One driver George Russell was one of his regular customers. Maybe. The guy did give me a great haircut and then talked me into letting him burn the little hairs off my ears with a fun process called ear flaming. He holds a flaming wand and quickly bounces it back and forth off your ears. Yes, really. It worked well and didn't seem to cause hearing loss, so I think the next time I'm in London I'll try to find that guy.

I followed up my fresh cut with a trip to Harrod's for a delicious ribeye steak lunch. I had been very light on the expense account to that point and felt like I could get away with one treat!

Next, I paid a visit to one of the royal parks. You may have read that all those flowers that were being placed in front of the gates at Buckingham Palace were carried over to the royal parks, where they were placed in bunches around the trees and other specific places. The smell of the fresh flowers that covered the ground for acres was overwhelming, with scents of roses, lilacs, and so many other types of flowers. The park was crammed full of people, some bringing more flowers, while others, like me, were just taking in the scene. Along with flowers, there were postcards, pictures, Union flags, and many other tokens of remembrance. A handmade card written with black Sharpie on cardboard said, "Thank you for all of your love, encouragement, and bright spirit that you have devoted all these years to the United Kingdom and the Commonwealth. You will be my inspiration now and forever. RIP My Queen!"

By the time I returned on Saturday night, my phone told me that I had walked fourteen miles. The Mad Day Out ended back at the Hilton, watching the BBC coverage of the preparations for the funeral that would take place on Monday.

The mood changed on Sunday. The seriousness of what was

about to happen seemed to be setting in. Eamonn Kelly is a popular presenter, or what we call a DJ, on one of the UK's most popular radio stations, and he's also a personal friend. On Sunday morning, I spoke with him about the feeling in London.

"Initial shock, I suppose. People just felt that the Queen would be here forever. We know that's an impossible thing, but she was the monarch for seventy years and the vast majority of people in the UK know nothing else but the Queen who has been here for that long," Kelly said. "Tens of thousands of people, if not hundreds of thousands now, have paid their respects and wanted to see the Queen lying in state, and I think that says everything."

Then I walked down Whitehall, one of the most important streets in all the United Kingdom as it houses many government offices. Number 10 Downing Street, the prime minister's residence, is just off Whitehall.

Hundreds of people sat on chairs along the sidewalk, prepared to stay more than twenty-four hours in order to have a front-row seat when the Queen's coffin passed by on a gun carriage. Some had traveled many miles to be there.

"We've come down here early this morning to get good position, on up the front, to be ready for the Queen's funeral tomorrow," Graham Ablett, camped out with wife Leslie, said. "Yeah, we've got everything, chairs, sleeping bags, rain cover to put over us so, we'll be out here in the elements, hoping we've got a good position for tomorrow. Being out all night is nothing to what she's done for us, really."

That really said it all. So many Brits feel that they owed it to Queen Elizabeth to pay their respects in person, and they were willing to put up with hardships and inconveniences to do just that.

Something unexpected happened that really struck me about why I was there and what this event in history meant. All of us in the media were upstairs at the Methodist Central Hall banging away on our laptops or doing live shots from the specially built platform. The Hall is still a functioning church, and Sunday services were taking place in the sanctuary. As I was sitting at my table, I heard a familiar song begin. I jumped up and ran over to the door of the balcony that overlooked the sanctuary. For the first time in seventy years, the congregation was standing to sing "God Save The King," the National Anthem of the United Kingdom, and for the last seventy years they had sung "God Save The Queen."

These are the same lyrics sung since at least 1745. The words ask for God's blessing over the monarch. As Americans, we don't necessarily understand the role of a monarch, and especially the relationship Queen Elizabeth had with her people. That week, I saw firsthand and learned that for many, it was sincere and heartfelt.

"I think a lot of people have been affected more than they thought by this," Eamonn Kelly had told me.

I found someone with a North Carolina connection that day. A former worker with Billy Graham's Samaritan's Purse organization was on the streets of London, ministering to those who were dealing with their emotions following the death of Queen Elizabeth II.

Mike Freeman had trained in North Carolina for disaster relief. "I was with the Billy Graham organization, and I was doing Samaritan's Purse and I was doing international relief work," Freeman said. Freeman was the coordinator of a group of street pastors. They spent hours walking the streets with the thousands of people who were "on the queue" for a look at the Queen's coffin inside Westminster Hall.

"We're with street pastors and response pastors and that's a ministry that goes out on the streets and we get alongside people, listening most importantly to their stories, listening to people," Freeman said. "Quite often for them, queuing for this lying-in-state brings more emotions to the forefront of perhaps their past losses and they want to talk about it, and we're a listening ear with compassion. We've got time to do that, and then we can encourage them to go on, and if we get the chance, we can share faith with them as well."

Just before heading out on Sunday morning, Freeman and another group of street pastors stopped to pray near Westminster Abbey. "People say, you know I've been in the queue twelve hours, fifteen hours, but I'd have queued twice as long just for that privilege of paying my respects for the Queen. Which is really great, because it helps them personally, and also as a nation we're showing respect for what was, in our lifetimes, our greatest monarch," Freeman told me. Rick and I spent a day of our own on the five-mile-long queue to see the coffin, walking along with some folks and talking with them about why they didn't mind waiting for hours. "I've never seen anything as long as this before," one man said. "We [British] love a queue."

Despite waiting and walking for nearly twenty-four hours, the behavior in the line seemed exceptionally polite.

"We don't push in," an elderly woman said. "We're very good." When asked if anyone ever tried to jump the queue, she replied, "Oh, they better not try. We did have one try, but we sorted that out."

"It will be worth it," Nancy Dove told me. "I think, the emotion, just to pay homage to a brilliant leader. Selfless. All giving. You can't say too much about her, and she really truly is Elizabeth the Great."

Two hosts of a popular British morning television show apparently managed to "jump the queue" and not wait. Once that information became public through the British tabloids, the reaction was one of rage.

One of my favorite moments in covering the days leading up to the funeral was meeting a man who was more than happy to wait his turn, even though he didn't have to. With his status, he could have gone into another line that would have gotten him to the front much more quickly. Nick Wilson is a wounded British Army veteran. Veterans were among those most determined to show their allegiance to the sovereign on the official days of mourning. Wilson told me he was grateful for the opportunity to see the Queen's coffin on the raised catafalque, adding that it was a fulfillment of the promise he made twenty-three years before. "I took an allegiance to serve Queen and Country back in 1999, and following that did multiple deployments in Northern Ireland, Kosovo, Iraq, and Afghanistan. And yeah, the Oath of Allegiance to any British veteran or service personnel is everything," Wilson said.

Wilson was at Westminster Hall with thousands of others, determined to pass by the coffin of his Queen. So many—veterans and civilians alike—wanted to come, that most streets in central London were shut down, and you could walk across London Bridge accompanied by a man playing bagpipes.

Right outside Westminster Palace, we met people leaving after having the briefest audience with the Queen. Some were sad, others pleased, but all seemed satisfied that they'd done it.

"It was awesome inside. It was like you're outside the real world and you're in a different world. Everything is so quiet, everybody was so respectful, the soldiers were so impressive, you couldn't forget that she was the Queen, you couldn't forget that she was our Queen," a woman told me.

And for Nick Wilson and millions more who wore the uniform in allegiance to the Queen and her realm, it was the chance to fulfill their pledge. " . . . and so being able to stand up, just about, and bang out a salute to her one more time, someone that I dedicated all of my life to." Wilson said.

But for some Britons, standing in queue wasn't how they chose to honor the Queen. Take Sally and Sue.

"We're sisters," they proudly told me.

They didn't live in London, but came to the capital to be near the activities. I found them enjoying a cup of tea at a small café near Westminster Abbey. Sue said that for a lot of Britons, just the act of coming to London was a homecoming. "I think because something like this brings the country together, makes me realize what a brilliant country it is and how we all come together at times like this and all support each other."

Sue didn't stand in the line this time, but did queue many years ago for another British hero. "I did for Winston Churchill," she said. "And while it was a different time and a different figure, the sentiment was the same. And there it is. There's the coffin. And in that case it was Winston Churchill, and you know a very important, momentous, significant person is lying there, and I think it will be the same for those seeing the Queen lie in state."

Sue said she was deeply affected by the Queen's death. She noted that even though Queen Elizabeth was ninety-six, the announcement of her death was still a shock, saying it is similar to when you know a loved one is at the point of death, but don't want to accept it. "We were in Cornwall at the time, and I remember it coming on the wireless and you're thinking no, that can't be so," she said. "You know they're ill, you know their time is nigh, you don't really believe it will happen, and I think it was the same with the Queen."

The state funeral took place at eleven o'clock on Monday. Rick and I were up and out of the hotel earlier than usual and had to skip that wonderful breakfast. We had to be inside the Methodist Central Hall by five. We flagged down a cab and when we told him where we needed to go, he just laughed, because he knew he wasn't going to be able to get us within three miles of where we needed to be due to the ring of security. He was right. He got us as close as he could and then we were on our own, lugging all of our equipment through very crowded streets and several checkpoints.

I've covered several presidential visits before and have seen tight security, but this was unlike anything I had ever experienced. Not only did you have London's Metropolitan Police, but officers from police agencies from across the United Kingdom, as well as a large presence from the British Armed Forces. And, with so many world leaders present, they each had their own security. Roads and sidewalks were closed, barriers were erected that stretched for blocks, sharpshooters were placed on the tops of buildings, helicopters surveyed the scene from above, and private security firms were employed with agents at every turn.

Rick and I were fortunate enough to have the proper credentials. The police issued a gold wristband with the block initials DCMS (Department for Culture, Media, and Sport) and the symbol of the monarchy. That wristband was truly the golden ticket that allowed us to have access everywhere, except inside Westminster Abbey.

From our perch at Methodist Central Hall, we watched the impressive procession make its way into the Abbey. The Royal Navy sailors pulled the gun carriage with Queen Elizabeth's coffin, topped by the crown, orb, and scepter. Members of the royal family walked behind. We also watched as world leaders and a few celebrities and other notables walked into the Abbey. The vast majority of the media saw the funeral exactly the same way millions of people across the world saw it: on a TV screen. In the CBS workspace, dozens stood around large screens. The silence in that usually busy temporary newsroom was broken only by the somber tone of the announcers and the voices of those who were speaking. I was watching the funeral in the same room and on the same monitor as national news anchors Norah O'Donnell and Gayle King from CBS. For a while, we were all just reporters who happened to be reporting on the biggest story in the world for that particular day.

Once the funeral ended and the world leaders had left Westminster Abbey, the security eased . . . a little bit. Rick and I had stories to put together using the video and voices from the funeral. As we started to work, I had an idea. I told Rick that I thought we should grab our gear and hit the streets to find some "real people" to interview. Yes, it would mean more work on an already tight deadline, but I knew it would make for better stories. There were thousands of people all around us who had been watching the funeral on TV in the pubs, on large screens set up in parks, or on their devices as they stood nearby.

"And I think that just shows how important she was, and she

went further than what people needed, she did more, she gave us what we didn't even realize we needed, which was fantastic," one woman told me.

After talking to several people, Rick and I went back inside the Methodist Central Hall and started working on the stories that we would present on the news Monday night. I felt a great responsibility to go over every word, every image, and every edit multiple times to make it as good as I possibly could. Because of the interest of so many news stations across the country, we did not have the luxury of time. We had to get the stories produced quickly. Things seemed to go well, other than the occasional technical hiccup, and I think we were both happy with what we got on air and online for our respective outlets.

I got back to the hotel after midnight and only managed a couple of hours of sleep before I had to get everything packed up and get in a cab to head to London's Heathrow Airport for an early morning flight back to Charlotte. All of my TV equipment I packed in a large suitcase, and even in these days of smaller cameras, the total of what I packed was way over the weight limit for flying free. When I lifted the suitcase onto the scales, I saw the eyes of the woman working for British Airways get very large. She looked at me and said, "You know this is very heavy, don't you?" I smiled at her and told her that yes, I knew that it was, adding that I didn't have a choice and would pay whatever I had to. She paused for a minute and then, to my great surprise, said, "Well, it's okay," and just let it go. I don't know what to attribute that act of kindness to, but I did appreciate it.

When I got home from our London adventure, I was overwhelmed with positive comments about our coverage, and that was very gratifying. My job had given me the opportunity to be an eyewitness to history and to describe it for our viewers back home, and that's something not many other jobs allow you to do. I will forever be grateful to those in our company that pushed to make this happen.

Afterword

Setting up my camera for my last live shot on the sidewalk outside of my bureau in Salisbury. December, 2023.

I SWITCHED OFF THE MICROPHONE AND POWERED DOWN my camera on December 14, 2023. My decision to retire had not been an easy one, but I knew it was the right thing to do.

Earlier in 2023, I was finishing up another of the ten three-year contracts I had with WBTV that spanned more than thirty years. I was going to meet with the news director to tell her about my decision to retire. She thought the meeting was for me to sign a new contract and was very surprised when I gave her this bit of news. Molly Dutton is a great news director and a good friend. I loved working for her. She has a family and understood the importance of a work/life balance in an industry where that often doesn't exist. We talked for a while, and she asked me to reconsider. I told her that I was firm in this decision, but at her request, I did agree to work about six weeks longer than I planned. The station was short-staffed at the time, and the November ratings period would begin soon. I also decided not to "phone it in" for the last few weeks, so I worked as hard as ever and tried to tell the best stories that I could.

Retiring at age sixty-two was a little earlier than I had originally planned. I often told people that I would work "until WBTV told me to stop," but circumstances involving friends and family members and a clear direction from God led me to move my retirement up by at least three years.

Too often, I've seen things happen to people that prevented them from enjoying their so-called "golden years" of a fulfilling retirement. My colleague and friend Steve Crump, hands down one of the best to ever report news in any market at any time, passed away from cancer while he was still working. WBTV meteorologist and friend Jason Myers and helicopter pilot and friend Chip Tayag, both under the age of fifty, died in a tragic helicopter crash. My brother Chris, who often talked about the things that he would do in his retirement, also passed away from complications related to cancer before he reached the age of sixty. Their stories, and many other similar ones, had me thinking that I should step away and try to enjoy as much of life as I could while I was still relatively young and healthy. I also wanted to spend more time with my granddaughters before they reached the stage in life where hanging out with the old man wouldn't be cool anymore.

As my last day at WBTV approached, I embarked on what seemed like a farewell tour with some of the people and stories that I had often reported on over the years. I was also humbled to be able to do some really fun things that involved both my job and my family. Charlotte Motor Speedway asked me to be the Grand Marshal for the annual Speedway Christmas light show. That's where you can drive through the track and be amazed at the sight of more than four million Christmas lights. It's very popular, and it's something I'd covered several times over the years. For the 2023 kickoff, I had my wife, son, daughter-in-law, and granddaughters on the track with me. WBTV also did a live broadcast for this event. My job was to officially turn on the lights, then drive a Toyota Camry pace car around the track, leading a long line of the first visitors along the course.

I got so excited about having this opportunity that I totally skipped the countdown! Instead, I did my live shot, threw my microphone to the photographer, then jumped in the car and did a tire-squealing burnout to head down the track, all with my wife in the front seat and my two granddaughters in the back seat having their first experience with g-forces. After about two hundred yards down the backstretch of the track, my wife yelled, "Slow down!" I dutifully took my foot off the gas, and we settled into a much safer speed to continue through the four-mile-long course. What a thrill! I even got a huge trophy and a checkered flag from the speedway for the reporting I had done over the years.

The farewell tour also included bringing the family along to turn on thousands of lights at the City of Kannapolis annual holiday celebration. There were also recognitions from the City of Salisbury, the Rowan County Commission, the Cabarrus Convention Visitors Bureau, the Rowan Economic Development Council, the Rowan Chamber, the Salisbury-Rowan Human Relations Council, the Salisbury Lions Club, and the unexpected awarding of the Order of the Long Leaf Pine, North Carolina's highest civilian honor. The recognition was truly rewarding, and it made me realize something that I had struggled with for decades: people genuinely noticed and appreciated the work I had done over thirty-two years.

There were many times that I'd come home from reporting and felt like my daily efforts had been pointless. I would work hard on a story that I thought was important and would receive little to no feedback. That led me to think that the things I worked on—the things I stressed out about and lost sleep over—didn't really matter in the lives of my viewers and readers. Yes, there would often be lots of comments on social media, but so many of them were negative that I just didn't pay much attention. In the last few weeks of my reporting career, though, I discovered there had been an appreciation for the stories I covered and for the way I did my job. It was the most gratifying time I have ever experienced.

I often had the opportunity to work with interns: high school or college students who expressed an interest in broadcast journalism. They would shadow me for a few days or a few weeks to see what the job was really like. Most of the interns I worked with did not choose a career in the field. They saw the long hours, missed holidays, and stress that comes with the job. Many young reporters that I trained had a similar experience. I was always disappointed with this outcome. I loved my job and was always enthusiastic about it, even when it called for self-sacrifice. It's not an easy job, and at least in the beginning, is not one that will put a big wad of money in your pocket. You'll have to deal with a lot of people who hate you, just because you represent "the media." Even so, it is rewarding in other ways that can sometimes take years to be evident. My hope is that young reporters will play the long game and realize that journalism is a noble calling that allows you to help those in the community that you serve. If you're just going into it to "be on TV," you probably won't make it. I did have the opportunity to train several other young reporters who now appear to be thriving, and that's good to see.

I would encourage you to support your local journalists and local media outlets. Whether it's TV, radio, newspaper, or online, these are the reporters who are in your community dutifully reporting on things that affect your life. Local reporters spend hours in city council and county commission meetings to find out about tax rates, school board issues, new economic development projects, and what's being done to curb crime where you live.

As I write this, we are in a changing landscape when it comes to media. Daily newspapers, in many cases, have become weekly, and newsrooms now employ a staff that is a fraction of what it was just a decade ago. Many social media sites claim they are a news organization, but are often just someone with an agenda who publishes unconfirmed and inaccurate information with no accountability. Your local journalists are watchdogs for local government. It's one of the most important functions that exists, and it's why the Founding Fathers placed such importance on freedom of the press.

God richly blessed me by allowing me to serve in this career for as long as I did. I'm grateful to viewers, readers, and listeners who allowed me to tell them a story. I had wonderful experiences, and I met people that I will never forget. I walk away with the satisfaction that what I was able to do made a positive difference, and that's about the best anyone can ask for.

About the Author

David Whisenant is an Emmy award-winning former television news reporter for CBS affiliate WBTV in Charlotte, North Carolina. He began his broadcasting career in radio in 1977 while he was a student at Salisbury High School. He became a full-time reporter for WBTV in 1994.

In his thirty-two years at WBTV, David covered major local and national stories, including covering the funerals of President Ronald Reagan and Queen Elizabeth II for WBTV and for affiliated television stations across the country. David has also filed reports for CBS News and the Weather Channel.

David retired from WBTV in December 2023. Following his retirement, David was awarded the Order of Long Leaf Pine, North Carolina's highest civilian honor. David is a 1983 graduate of Appalachian State University. He is married to Jtan and they have a son, Kyle, daughter-in-law Anna, and granddaughters Ava and Maisie. David is a deacon and Sunday School teacher at First Baptist Church in Salisbury.

Printed in the USA
CPSIA information can be obtained
at www.ICGtesting.com
CBHW040414101224
18740CB00012B/102